RUSSIA

HEILONGJIANG

Morin Dawa
Daurzu Zizhiqi

Hailar

Qiqihar

HARBIN

CHANGCHUN

JILIN

MONGOLIA

INNER MONGOLIA

Hinggan Mountains

LIAONING

SHENYANG

NORTH KOREA

Sea of Japan

JAPAN

Hami

HOHHOT

BEIJING
BEIJING

Bohai Sea

SOUTH KOREA

Korea Strait

Dunhuang

TIANJIN

HEBEI

Yellow

SHIJIAZHUANG

Yellow Sea

Aksai County

YINCHUAN

SHANXI

TAIYUAN

GANSU

QILIAN SHAN

NINGXIA

SHANDONG

JIANGSU

Huizu County

ZHENGZHOU

QAIDAM PENDI

XINING

LANZHOU

XI'AN

SHAANXI

HENAN

ANHUI

NANJING

SHANGHAI

Golmud

Labrang

HEFEI

HANGZHOU

QINGHAI

ANYEMAQEN SHAN

Maqu

Zoige

HUBEI

ZHEJIANG

East China Sea

Heyan

BAYAN HAR MOUNTAINS

Songpan

WUHAN

Yushu

Serxu

Hongyuan
Heishui

Zadoi

Manigango

Serta

Barkham

Dege

Ganzi

Jinchuan

CHENGDU

HANCHANG

JIANGXI

FUJIAN

FUZHOU

TAIPEI

MOUNTAINS

Riwoqe

Danba

SICHUAN

CHANGSHA

Batang

Yajiang

HUNAN

Namjagbarwa

Bomi

Litang

Kangding

Minya Gongga

LHASA

Mainling

Markham

Yanjing

Daocheng

Zayu

Deqen

Muli

GUIZHOU

TAIWAN

Cona

Zhongdian

Panzhihua

Yulongxueshan

Xundian

GUIYANG

GUANGDONG

Brahmaputra River

Lijiang

KUNMING

GUANGXI

GUANGZHOU

Dali

Hong Kong

DESH

YUNNAN

NANNING

Taiwan Strait

Pacific Ocean

MYANMAR
(BURMA)

Salween River

VIETNAM

Beibu Gulf

HAIKOU

South China Sea

PHILIPPINES

LAOS

HAINAN

A "funnel" in the Arjin Shan
Nature Reserve, where fresh
water emanates from the foot of a
massive sand dune into a rushing
river. Note the man at left.

The 119,300 members of the Jingpo nationality in Santaishan, south-western Yunnan, are related to the Kachin of northern Burma. Here they parade to the Mulou-zhong call of the local headman, which once represented either preparation for battle or a victory celebration. Today, these events celebrate a good harvest at the Mulouzhong Festival, on the 15th day of the First Moon. Group danc-ing and singing sometimes involves several thousand people. Wooden drums, gongs, cymbals and bamboo flutes accompany the festivities. Animists, the Jingpo believe that spirits inhabit trees, rocks, animals, and the sun, moon and stars, and thus are careful not to anger them.

The Bai nationality consists of almost 1.6 million people. Living along the shores of Lake Erhai in Dali, Yunnan, many Bai ply the lake's waters in traditional junks, using nets to fish for a living. Some Bai people train cormorants to catch fish in the winter as well.

Khartan River Valley in Aksai
County, a few hours' drive south
of Dunhuang.

In Heishui, Jiarong Tibetans spread corn to dry on balconies and eaves. The corn is used mainly as animal feed in this earthquake-prone area. Stepladders, hewn from a single log, connect levels of their homes and are more common than staircases as we know them. Stairs can be quite steep at a 35-degree angle, with the log ladders angled at 60 degrees or more. Such ladders are used in defense towers as well, since no entrance exists at ground level. Jiarong Tibetans are predominantly agriculturalists, raising some sheep, goats and yaks. Scholars believe that the language they speak closely resembles ancient Tibetan.

A Class One protected animal, the rare wild yak is limited to remote regions of the Tibetan Plateau, including Xinjiang's Arjin Shan Nature Reserve. Adult bulls stand 1.8 meters (5.9 ft) high, have formidable horns spanning up to one meter (3.3 ft) and can weigh over a ton (907 kg, or 2,000 lb). Experts estimate that about 15,000 wild yak remain today, thriving above altitudes of 4,000 meters (13,123 ft).

Wild yaks (*Bos grunniens*) are usually completely black, while their domestic counterparts range from grey to white to black. However, a startling mutation has occurred in the wild—golden yaks. Wildlife biologist George Schaller first published this observation, citing that one to two percent of wild yaks in Tibet's Aru region were completely golden. I too have seen wild golden yaks, including calves, in Qinghai province's Aksai Autonomous Kazak County.

A QUARTER CENTURY OF EXPLORATION

FROM MANCHURIA TO TIBET

PHOTOGRAPHY BY

WONG HOW MAN

Foreword by Francesca von Habsburg

Text by **Wong How Man** with Julie Gaw

Distribution in the United States of America by
W. W. Norton & Company, Inc., New York

Published by Odyssey Publications Limited
1004 Kowloon Centre, 29–43 Ashley Road,
Tsim Sha Tsui, Kowloon, Hong Kong
Tel: (852) 2856 3896   Fax: (852) 2565 8004
E-mail: odyssey@asiaonline.net

98 99 00 01 02   5 4 3 2 1

Distribution in the United Kingdom, Ireland and Europe by
Hi Marketing Ltd, 38 Carver Road, London SE24 9LT, UK

Library of Congress Catalog Card Number has been requested.

ISBN 962-217-098-6

Editorial Coordinator: Julie Gaw
Editors: Christine Headley and Pamela Logan
Design: Margaret Lee
Maps: Mark Stroud

Colour separations by Daiichi System Graphics Company Ltd
Printed in Hong Kong by Paramount Printing Company Ltd

PREVIOUS PAGE At a height of 3,785 meters (12,418 ft), a monk shovels snow from the roof of Palpung Gonpa (Babang Monastery) to prevent water damage. The two structures on the roof provide ventilation, with the platform on the right an altar for burning offerings of juniper branches. The typically Tibetan stepladder is hewn from a single log. Built of interlocking logs, the structure is highly resistant to the earthquakes that frequently rock the region, as they have in 1976, 1981 and 1995. Granite mountains in the shape of three sacred elephants playing in the water—a reference to Buddhist scripture—lie beyond, making this an auspicious location for the monastery, despite the earthquakes.

ACKNOWLEDGEMENTS

As I turn 50, my father turns 80, and my son 20. Each of us is 30 years apart. I thank my father for the cultivation of my diverse interests, by providing an example through his own passion in both science and the arts. He is a man of fine scholarship, distinguished by a life-long career of teaching science, combined with his cherished extra-curricular activities, which include the adaptation of contemporary Cantonese operas into English.

As for my son Kaigee, he began his exploration career when he was eight months old, on my backpack to Inner Mongolia, riding camels and living in a *yurt*. He joined my second expedition to the source of the Yangtze in 1995, giving me the chance to teach him what my father taught me: "When drinking water, think of the source," a revelation of ancient Chinese piety for our heritage and roots. Oigee, my daughter, continues our Chinese heritage by studying Mandarin, despite having been born and raised in the United States.

I thank my mother for offering me the opportunity since childhood to be defiant and do the extraordinary, yet with the ability to circumvent her disciplinary action. Her constant instilling of values upheld my moral responsibility, preventing me from straying too far from the norm. This culminated into a balance between exploration for personal satisfaction, while conserving and restoring some of the damage man has left behind to our natural and cultural heritage.

I thank my wife, Chen Li, for the last ten years of support, both in spirit and in actual work in the field. Despite her physical weaknesses, she stood by my side through some of the more difficult years, when funds were scanty and workload excessive. Giving up her successful career as a performing artist in China, she helped collect many utilitarian objects of the indigenous peoples, and video-taped the dances and rituals of vanishing cultures.

The long list of thanks to those who have helped me achieve a quarter century of exploration in China could fill several pages. I can name but a few here and apologize for the many omissions. Thanks to the National Geographic for honing my exploration skills. And a huge "thank you" to supporters of the China Exploration and Research Society, in particular Daniel Ng and John Farrell, for giving me the vehicle to go beyond exploration into conservation for future generations. I thank Kathy Young, Cathy Hilborn and Berry Sin, for dedicating their time and service to our cause.

I would like to acknowledge the support of Kodak; the visual results are shown in the photographs of this book. I also thank my many corporate sponsors, among them Shell, The Hongkong Bank, Coca-Cola and Land Rover, who have given me years of continuous support.

I thank my close friend Francesca von Habsburg for her eloquent Foreword. Magnus Bartlett is more than a publisher, but a dear friend for almost as long as my work life in China. Had it not been for his forbearance upon a delinquent author, this book may have become a half-century rather than 25-year account.

I would like to thank William Bleisch for inspiring me to work with wildlife. I thank Pam Logan, whom I derailed from being an aerospace scientist into becoming a China explorer, and in turn used her scientific discipline to assist my organization. I appreciate Margaret Lee's excellent work in designing this book. Thanks are due Julie Gaw for collating much of my archives into comprehensive order, and helping turn this book into reality.

Wong How Man
August 18, 1998
Hong Kong

CONTENTS

This arid, lunar landscape appeared north
of Ali, Tibet's most westerly prefecture,
after ten days of driving across the northern
Changtang plateau.

1. Elaborate collar of turquoise and beads on Tibetan woman at Koko-nor (Qinghai Lake).

2. Jiarong Tibetan woman in Heishui, Sichuan.

3. Necklace of coral—part of the bride price—for a newlywed Tajik in the Chinese Pamirs.

4. Familiar Tibetan pattern on the fringe of a man's jacket, Qinghai Lake.

5. Lhoba sword and shell belt in Mainling, southeastern Tibet.

6. Braids decorated with amber, at Serxu's summer horse racing festival.

7. Jiarong woman's belt displays fine embroidery and silver.

8. Ceremonial rattan headdress with boar's tooth and feathers, worn by Jingpo men during their annual festival parade.

9. A Tibetan nomad (*drokpa*) faces life with essential items on his person, including an amulet-like charm box around his neck for protection (*gawo*), knife and flint pouch.

10. The Oroqen of Manchuria use birch bark boxes as sewing kits and storage pouches.

11. Woolen boots, with soles of undressed yak hide, on Khampa man near Gartok, the capital of Markam, southeastern Tibet.

FOREWORD

It is rare to find someone as sensitive to so many diverse aspects of his heritage as Wong How Man—by nature an explorer and by choice a unique conservationist, in both the cultural and ecological sense. Since he made me promise not to write much flowery praise of him, I have no choice but to tell about the goals we both share and implement in our respective work on two distant continents.

Although he specifically wanted me to write about my experiences in Asia, this is unfair; they would pale in comparison to the wonderfully rich stories he describes in this beautiful book. However, I will mention that experiencing the traditions and cultures of foreign lands and distant religions helped me become more devoted to my own faith. I now experience to the fullest joys of my European cultural roots, which I had previously taken completely for granted. It was during this spiritual and physical journey abroad that I became so passionate about the world's cultural heritage. It affects our present existence as well as the future we choose to define for ourselves, and for our children's children.

How Man and I are both advocates of conservation, which makes us dedicated to the future. How could we ever pretend to be interested in the future if we were to neglect the past? We have long established that looking after our planet is the single most important thing we can do, not only for ourselves but also for generations to come. It constantly puzzles conservationists like us, why is the preservation of our global heritage *not* directly linked to the generous sense of responsibility we all already share? Are these two things not inextricably linked though time? Are they both not the custodians of our past, embodying all knowledge and materia that defines what we have become, and how we got here?

What I admire most about How Man's work with the China Exploration & Research Society is his meticulous attention to detail. His multi-disciplinary approach covers such a broad scope of interest, which is vital to understanding ourselves. He understands all aspects of a region, from the flora and fauna to the various layers of civilization which have interacted with that environment over the centuries, even when that influence is no longer present. He celebrates this persevering survival in this book, sharing and emphasizing a world that *is*, not was. Through his tireless work, How Man will positively impact the world's respect not only of nature but also of people, their traditions and the cultural heritage they value so tremendously. A tolerant future is a world full of people willing to respect each other's identities. An understanding of the future is a profound respect of the past.

Francesca von Habsburg
April 12, 1998

1

2

3

1. Lisu man of southwestern China.

2. A Jiarong Tibetan woman of Songpan, Sichuan wears her hair in 108 plaits, adorned with yellow amber.

3. Tibetan yak herder near the foothills of Anye Maqen Mountain.

4. Washi Golok nomad boy of Litang, southwestern Sichuan.

5. Tibetan woman with elaborate amber, turquoise and coral jewelry.

6. Man of the Hui nationality in Lanzhou, Gansu.

7. Dulong woman from along the upper Salween River. It is believed that women with distinctive facial tattoos are less susceptible to being kidnapped by neighboring clans.

8. Kazak boy near Tianchi, Xinjiang.

4

5

6

7

8

INTRODUCTION

Nearly two hundred years ago Napoleon is alleged to have said, "China is a sleeping giant, let it stay asleep, for when it wakes up, it will shake the world." On October 1, 1949, that prophecy was fulfilled. With a resounding voice, Mao Tse-tung stood in Beijing's Tiananmen Square to declare, "The Chinese people have stood up!"

Five weeks prior to Mao's famous proclamation, I was born in the then-British colony of Hong Kong. In many ways I grew up in tandem with the young nation, my birthdays reminders of the age of new China.

Indeed, even my style of operation in China owes much to the heritage of the new government. By adopting bold tactics not unlike the indomitable guerilla army of Mao's Long March, I have been able to explore, and later on conduct research and conservation projects, in remote regions that others find difficult to penetrate. My inspiration came from both my Chinese heritage and Western education.

My elementary education was in a Christian school that had moved from Guangdong (Canton) to Hong Kong after the Communist Revolution. The Jesuits, who operated my middle school, also had a long history on the mainland through their missionary work. But it wasn't until I entered university, in Wisconsin USA, that I began to identify deeply with China. Throughout college, I sought to understand better my heritage, avidly reading about China's geography, history, art and culture, both past and present.

I learned that in the Far East, we too have our share of great explorers, whose exploits rivaled if not surpassed those like Christopher Columbus and Marco Polo. Tang dynasty pilgrim monk Xuan Zang, Ming travel writer Xu Xiake and the Chinese Muslim admiral Cheng He are explorers familiar to Chinese children. Combing the library stacks, I also learned about Westerners who took advantage of turmoil in the late Qing dynasty to explore China's remote frontiers. These 20th-century explorers—Prejevalsky, Younghusband, Stein, Hedin, Andrews, Lattimore and Rock—inspired me with their vivid tales of adventure and discovery.

Being Chinese, I have had the opportunity to explore remote regions of China for the last quarter century, arcing across the country from Manchuria in the northeast, through Inner Mongolia and Xinjiang, to Tibet and beyond. My journalism background gave me the great fortune to work under the auspices of the National Geographic Society, and to address the Royal Geographical Society on several occasions. By the standards of my predecessors, and possibly those coming after me, my discoveries are quite modest. Yet they are nonetheless important to me.

The year 1999 marks the 50th anniversary of the People's Republic of China. It also marks my 50th birthday, and perhaps more importantly, the 25th anniversary of my first trip into China. My explorations began during Easter 1974, several months after graduating from university. That first year alone, I made three journeys to the mainland.

At the time, China was just starting to unveil itself, like a new bride, to the West. Most newspaper reports were rosy and positive. With Nixon's historic visit just two years earlier, the US and China were enjoying their honeymoon.

Red China, as it was then called, left a deep impression on me—sometimes more emotional than rational. The regimentation of adults and children alike was adulated as fine discipline. The turbulence of political rallies near the end of the Cultural Revolution was interpreted as dynamism. At the end of my trips, I even submitted with little question to having my exposed film left behind, processed and inspected, before it was sent on to Hong Kong.

As a young and aspiring journalism graduate, I took many photographs, within the constraints of my limited budget, wherever I went. My first camera was a Nikon bought after months of saving. Never did it cross my mind that these pictures might, in time, become a record of history, of China in transition, as well as a record of my own life's involvement with a country I've learned to love. Eighty thousand frames later, it is rather exciting to revisit the first roll of slides I took in China 25 years ago.

During those early years, the West knew nothing of China's rugged outback, places sealed to the outside world. I went through coastal China, all the way to the northeast. An interest in art, culture, and architecture helped win me several assignments for *Architectural Digest*. In 1979, one of these assignments took me to Inner Mongolia, in the country's far north. I was to study and write about the history of a unique human habitat: the movable Mongolian home called a *yurt*. Thus began my exploration path of no return.

My exposure to the *yurt* and Mongolian lifestyle not only opened me to the huge horizons of the northern steppe, but also unlocked a new fascination with exploration that would keep me occupied for decades to come. I came to realize the immense diversity of Chinese geography and ethnic culture yet found scanty information available to help me better understand these areas. The few books I found were usually outdated. It dawned on me that I was in a unique position to fill that vacuum of knowledge.

My subsequent work in southwestern Yunnan province and the Tibetan Plateau attracted the notice of the National Geographic Society, which began to support my work in 1982. In all, I led six NGS expeditions that helped to define my later work. Picture editor Mary Smith and text editor William Graves helped chart my career as a photographer/writer. With their support, I began to probe farther and farther into the Chinese outback.

During my third assignment for the National Geographic, I explored the sensitive border of Manchuria, land of northeast China bordering what was then the Soviet Union. The two Communist powers skirmished as recently as 1969. The frontier was now quiet, and my focus was not political. I was interested in two groups of nomadic hunters, the Ewenki and the Oroqen people. I had to be there during the long and bitter winter, when hunting activities were in full swing.

By that time in 1983, I had visited and studied at least half of China's 55 recognized ethnic groups, most of whom still strongly upheld their traditional culture. But in Manchuria, I was shocked to find that the hunting culture was on the verge of disappearing. Indeed, the liberation and later liberalization of China has been a dual-edged sword: while economic conditions of indigenous people are improving, the social fabric once so important to their community is slowly disintegrating.

A brief account of some of my encounters on expeditions will shed light on my gradual evolution from explorer to conservationist. In the winters of 1983 and 1988, I recorded the following in Manchuria:

The LCD display on my watch had long gone into hibernation as the mercury dropped to -40°C. We are camping in the snow. My sleeping bag is only rated to -30°. A campfire provides the extra ten degrees insulation—a slim margin between being frozen and barely warm.

With me is Lajimi, who is representative of the diversity of China's frontiers. He speaks Chinese, Russian, Japanese and Ewenki, which is his mother tongue, a dialect of Tungus. During the 20th century his land has been ruled by Manchus, Russians, the Chinese Republic, Japanese, numerous warlords with no allegiance to anyone, and now the Communist government. At the time of my visit, all that remained of his people, the Yagut, were 166 individuals.

Traditionally nomadic hunters, the Yagut move about in pursuit of game, using reindeer as pack animals to carry their camps across the forests of the Hinggan Mountains. Their homes are tipi-like structures, similar to those used by some American Indians. The walls are lined with birch bark during summer, and fur during the bitter winters.

Recently, the encroaching logging industry has decimated the animals on which the Yagut depended for their livelihood. Shrieks of the loggers' chainsaws have obliterated the songs of the hunters and the quiet whisper of their traditional jew's-harp. Today the Yagut do less and less hunting. The reindeer are no longer beasts of burden; instead their antlers are harvested when still covered in velvet, which is highly valued as an aphrodisiac.

Lajimi sharpens his knife and picks up a piece of scrap wood lying on the ground. Then he fashions for me an elaborate weapon resembling a crossbow. In the past, such devices were set upon the forest floor where animals frequently passed. A triggering device released the deadly arrow. I asked for a demonstration and Lajimi replied with a sigh, "It is far too dangerous. There are many passers-by today, and they do not know the forest at all."

Lajimi then demonstrates how to make a drinking bowl and a match container, using freshly cut birch bark. But bowls of porcelain or plastic, gas lighters and other gadgets of the modern world have all but replaced these utilitarian and ritualistic objects, once made with skill and pride. The last birch bark canoe I saw in 1983 has disappeared in 1988.

Niuna, the last Shaman, holds the remaining key to the Yagut's religious past. I interviewed her extensively with the help of an interpreter, her daughter Nanina. I asked her to re-enact the ritual shamanistic dance. Citing the lack of the shaman's drum and elaborate costume, she could no longer enter into a trance. With the passing of this last generation, the story of the Yagut may become only a small footnote in the history of Manchuria.

Much has been said about endangered wildlife. Lajimi and his culture are, without question, a more threatened species than the tigers and sables he used to hunt in the dense forests of the Hinggan Mountains. The plight of the Yagut mirrors the situation of the neighboring Oroqen, Daur and Manchu people, unless some concrete measures are taken to preserve their culture and environment.

Perhaps my most important contribution to geographic knowledge is my exploration of the Yangtze River. In 1985, my team compared two likely sources of the Yangtze: Tuotuohe at the glaciers of Geladandong Mountains to the west, and Dam Qu at a high alpine meadow to the east. With the aid of images made from space, I deduced that Dam Qu is a longer and thus more important source of the great river, despite its less dramatic scenery. But the debate continues among Chinese geographers, notwithstanding that no other team has actually inspected both sources. One of my proudest moments came when I stood at the source of the Yangtze, with one foot on each bank, and drank from the trickling flow. I wrote, "The water was freezing, but it warmed my heart."

In 1987 the China Exploration and Research Society was founded to advance exploration and archive materials I had collected. Thus, I work directly with a team of Chinese scientists to promote both cultural and wildlife conservation. In 1995, I led a CERS team back to the Yangtze's source to verify and expand my earlier work. A partial excerpt from my diary entry for the day at the source of Dam Qu is perhaps worth rendering here:

Awake 6:50 a.m. -3.7°C inside tent. Altitude 4,760 meters (15,616 feet). Clear sky. Headache all night. Felt better at 9 a.m. after two aspirins.

10 a.m. overcast. Left camp toward source at 11:30. Followed Dam Qu to small creek. Arrived source at 12:30. Water oozed from puddle 100 meters-plus from below source of 1985, reflecting two years of drought. Local nomads called the hill "Golden Plate," as rocks along river are colored with orange moss. Collected water, rocks and botanical samples. Buried Yangtze CD-ROM at 32° 45.15'N 94° 36.05'E. Altitude 4,820 meters (15,813 feet). Hiked up to ridge of watershed at 4,980 meters (16,338 feet). Saw herd of Tibetan gazelle. Began hailing, then snowing, at ridge. Returned to camp at 5 p.m.

A decade has passed, the water is still freezing, and it still warms my heart.

Following the discovery of a new source for the Yangtze, I began to include nature conservation in my work. In this phase of my career, the Arjin Mountain Nature Reserve in Xinjiang province offers the greatest challenge. The Arjin Mountain range marks an important divide between two important and massive ecosystems, that of the Tibetan Plateau and the Taklamakan Desert. Animals of both regions are found within the reserve, including rare species like the wild yak, wild ass, Tibetan antelope, gazelles, argali sheep and blue sheep. Some of these ungulates appear in extremely large herds, as up to 4,000 animals have been seen together at one time.

Between 1991 and 1998, I visited the Arjin Mountains four times. Each time the splendor and wildlife captivated me. Yet the diminishing number of animals alarmed me. Our exploration and research efforts within the Arjin Mountains have yielded many important results, especially after I became Chief Advisor for the reserve in 1993. Seeking to publicize the decimation of animal populations, I reported:

Zhang Huibin is the Deputy Reserve Chief and our collaborator on wildlife research. His account of the magnitude of illegal poaching activities at the Arjin Mountain reserve sheds light on the size of these rare resources. In recent

years, the most coveted wildlife of the entire plateau is the Tibetan antelope or chiru. Its superior wool is considered the most prized cashmere, called shah-toosh. *It is woven into the finest shawl, fit for royalty in India and the West. An entire shawl is fine enough to be pulled through a finger ring.*

Each antelope can yield only about 100 grams of such cashmere wool. Historically, they are traded through the Himalayas into India in small quantities. But times have changed. New wealth has created an insatiable market, offsetting the old balance of supply and demand. Today, poachers equipped with modern firearms and four-wheel-drive vehicles travel into the Arjin Mountains in pursuit of rare wild game. The number of antelopes taken over the last few years is phenomenal and the population is in rapid decline.

While my work in exploration has been somewhat eclipsed by my conservation endeavors, it remains in my heart to return some day exclusively to exploration and research. The China Exploration and Research Society's role in conservation is merely temporary until China is able to devote more resources, commensurate with its economic growth, and is better equipped to take up these matters as a national priority. I hope that future generations will have far more vision—insight as well as hindsight—to take care of our common cultural and natural heritage.

Wong How Man
August 15, 1998

1. Jiarong nomad woman of Heishui with embroidered headdress.

2. Khampas like this *bashi* (caravan leader) are renowned for their legendary military prowess.

3. Uygur girl of Da Mazar, southern Xinjiang.

4. Tibetan nomad from Maqu, Gansu, at religious festival.

5. Pancho Lemji, village chief in northwestern Tibet's Rutog (Rutok) County, was a Chinese guide during the 1962 border conflict with India.

6. Khampa man of Moyun. Note the fleece of his sheepskin jacket.

7. Tibetan man and child.

8. Khampas typically wear head-dresses of red yarn, with turquoise and ivory rings attached.

9. Xindong, a 72-year-old Lhoba and respected leader of the Bugar'er tribe at Mainling, southern Tibet, displays traditional hunting gear. His rattan helmet, lined with bearskin, may serve as camouflage on the hunt.

10. Pilgrim woman circumambulating Jokhang temple in Lhasa, capital of Tibet.

MANCHURIA
INNER MONGOLIA

With the Great Wall as testimony to the struggle to keep "barbarians" out of the Middle Kingdom, there is no doubt that the Chinese viewed Manchu and Mongol peoples of the northern steppe as a threat. In Manchuria, these indigenous peoples included not only the powerful Manchus, who conquered China in the 17th century and established the Qing dynasty (1644–1911), but also smaller, forest-dwelling groups of Ewenki and Oroqen. Similarly, the Mongols, who captured Beijing in 1267 under Kublai Khan and ruled China as the Yuan dynasty (1271–1368), share their vast grasslands with other nationalities such as the Tu and Yugur.

Manchuria previously consisted of 19 provinces, which the Chinese Communist government realigned in 1956 as the provinces of Heilongjiang, Jilin and Liaoning, plus the eastern flank of Inner Mongolia. Russian and Japanese forces struggled for control of Manchuria in the late 19th and early 20th century, leading to dramatic border shifts at China's expense. The area considered Manchuria today covers 1,554,000 sq km (600,000 sq mi) and is home to more than 95 million people. The land is heavily forested and possesses vast oil and mineral resources.

The Mongols—descendants of Genghis Khan's vast warrior hordes—inhabit both the now-independent Republic of Mongolia and the part of China designated as Inner Mongolian Autonomous Region, with Russia to the north and Han-dominated provinces to the south. On this cool, dry, sparsely populated steppe, pastoral nomadism rules; livestock such as sheep and goats provide sustenance. The Manchus annexed Inner Mongolia in 1635. Today's Inner Mongolian Autonomous Region, at 1.2 million sq km (460,000 sq mi), occupies fully one eighth of China's land area, and is home to 21.5 million people, of whom roughly one quarter are ethnic Mongolian.

LEFT   In camp, skis line a snowbank while reindeer forage in the distance. A blazing fire hardly keeps off the chill. The temperature that night dropped to -40°C (-40°F), my coldest night ever of open camping!

ABOVE   A revered hunter of the Ewenki nationality, Lajimi glides through the forest on birch skis in 1983. His pants, jacket and boots are made of moose hide, which also lines the bottom of his skis. The hairs, pointing backwards, reduce friction and provide traction on snow-covered slopes. Such ingenuity reflects a nearly vanished hunting-based economy. Ewenki men once stalked wildlife in winter, when fur was at its most luxurious, and Ewenki women tanned hides. The Ewenki live in a commune called Hui, over 150 km (93 mi) north of Hailar in Inner Mongolia.

PREVIOUS PAGE   Ewenki men in Manchuria.

ABOVE Both the saddlebags and harness of this domestic reindeer are made from moose hide. Its Yagut owners will harvest the antlers when they next come into velvet. Unlike several deer species, both male and female reindeer grow antlers and shed them on a yearly basis.

RIGHT Niuna was the sole shaman among the Yagut people in 1983. While members of either sex could become a shaman, Yagut usually chose women for this combined position of magician, dream interpreter, fortune teller, astrologer and healer. When asked to demonstrate her centuries-old, animistic rituals, Niuna looked despondent. Lacking her old shaman's costume of a decorated moose-skin smock and headdress like a reindeer's harness, along with her drum and spirit stick, Niuna felt powerless to get in touch with the animistic world. Yagut animistic beliefs closely resemble those of the Mongols.

The word "shaman," which has its origin in the Manchu-Tungus tongue, means an "agitated, frenzied person." This might seem strange, but the term is logical if one considers the type of persons eligible for the office of a shaman. The position was neither hereditary nor elective. One had to fall within one of the three following categories: Persons born with the afterbirth (foetal membrane) intact; persons who recovered from a long and apparently fatal illness; or persons who had had epileptic fits, with a gnashing of teeth and uncontrollable spasms and ravings.
—Qiu Pu, 1983

ABOVE Moose hooves on the tanned hide salt bag act as a rattle, which Yagut women use to call their domestic reindeer. Knowing they will get a treat of salt, the reindeer come running. Their usual winter diet of moss and lichen provides inadequate salt intake. When hunting, Yagut men spread salt on the ground and then lie in wait for wild animals to gather at the salt lick.

LEFT Capable of shouldering up to 50 kg (110 lb) for long distances, reindeer regularly transport children.

19

Standing 1.2 meters (4 ft) tall at the shoulder and weighing up to 136 kg (300 lb), reindeer (*Rangifer tarandus*) forage beneath the snow for food. Rare, pure white reindeer hold great religious significance among the Yagut.

LEFT Women prepare reindeer for a hunting excursion. The tipi-like structure, called *xierenzhu* in Chinese, used to house the Yagut year-round. Traditionally covered with birch bark in summer and animal hides in winter, today's *xierenzhu* are covered in canvas.

ABOVE During a Yagut hunt, Alexander mimics the call of a stag by drawing air into this horn of birch wood and fish glue. Upon hearing this sound, male deer believe that another stag has violated his territory and thus rush toward the intruder. Blowing on the opposite end of the horn approximates the low bellow of the moose.

The Yagut traditionally practiced ice fishing as a supplement to their hunting activities, but this was becoming rare during my visit in 1983. Yagut also used to harvest caviar from sturgeons for sale to international markets. A unique, traditional Yagut fishing net I collected in 1983 has many small pieces of birch bark attached to it.

Yagut hunting excursions earlier this century annually yielded thousands of squirrels to be traded with the Russians. Yagut also hunted sable, otter, deer, moose and bear. Believing they were descended from bears, the Yagut hold the animal in high esteem. In tune with the natural environment around them, Yagut hunters have recognized that squirrel and sable populations maintain an inversely proportional relationship: when squirrel populations soar, sable numbers diminish, and vice versa.

The forests of northeastern China previously sustained Yagut hunting activities. In 1925, Adachi Kinnosuke noted that more than 45 million acres—roughly one fifth of the total area of Manchuria—remained forested, from which loggers could harvest 150 million cubic feet of timber. With increased logging activities, wildlife numbers have decreased markedly; hunting is on the decline.

ABOVE LEFT   Yagut men relax inside their canvas-covered, tipi-like home.

ABOVE RIGHT   A Suolun man, wearing a sheepskin jacket, enjoys a draw on his pipe.

OPPOSITE PAGE   An extended Suolun family pose in front of the *yurt* they call home. Young Suolun women like to wear robes of blue cloth, bound at the waist with a yellow sash.

FOLLOWING PAGES   Hunters of a bygone era, the Suolun have turned to pastoral nomadism like their Mongol neighbors. This largest sub-group of the Ewenki at 85 percent (15,000 members in 1983), the Suolun live in *yurts* and raise livestock. Here the Suolun of Hui commune herd a large flock of sheep to market. The richest families in this region owned up to 700 sheep in the early 1980s. Most Suolun live in the Ewenki Autonomous Banner of the Morindawa Daur Autonomous Banner, in the Inner Mongolian Autonomous Region.

Mongolia and Manchuria are the original home of the ponies which are world-beaters in their power of endurance and their ability to survive on coarse and scanty feed. The near-World Empire of the great Kublai Khan was founded on the Mongolian pony. There is very little fable about this statement. It was the great Khan's cavalry, and not his infantry, which swept everything before it far beyond the Danube. It was mounted on the Mongolian pony. He is small; his low forelegs, high stern, and comparatively long trunk make him no prize-winner at a beauty show. But when the whole world is fast locked in ice and an arctic blizzard tunes up over a thousand-mile stretch of snow-whitened Manchurian and Mongolian steppes, his shaggy and stubborn form has all the appearances of a world-conqueror. The least tribute one can pay him is to say that he is the ancestor of practically all north-Asian horses.

—Adachi Kinnosuke, 1925

A third Ewenki sub-group, the Tungus, numbered 3,000 in 1983. They combine hunting and herding to eke out a living. Tungus people are reputed to be excellent warriors and hunt on horseback.

LEFT Living in the Hinggan Mountain Range in Heilongjiang province near China's northeastern border with Russia, the Oroqen comprise one of China's smallest nationalities with about 7,000 people. A traditional hunter, this man wears a camouflage hat made with the head of a yearling roebuck.

MIDDLE While the men hunt, Oroqen women skin and tan animal hides. They embroider traditional designs reflecting natural motifs on wolf skins, and use roe deer antlers to carve intricate patterns on birch bark sewing boxes. Oroqen women also look after the health and well-being of their family, tend the fire and manage food in their traditional tipi-like homes.

RIGHT An Oroqen boy kisses his younger sibling, swaddled in a hanging birch bark cradle. The cradle protects against the potential dangers of a nomadic camp, from campfires to wild animals. In the past, mothers nursed their babies while they remained safely in their cradles. The toddler's roe deer hat, previously worn only by hunters, symbolizes the hope that he will grow up to become a good hunter.

OPPOSITE PAGE An extended Oroqen family at home.

The Oroqen hunters were well acquainted with the lay of the land and rarely lost their way... To them, a south wind in winter was a sign of snow; yellowish clouds meant drought, and a haze in summer with midges flying meant rain. They discovered that just as wind direction was important to hunting so were seasonal changes, storms and lightning, clear skies and cloudy skies, and the waxing and waning of the moon... All this experience was gradually enriched and handed down from generation to generation. Every Oroqen male was trained to be a hunter from earliest childhood.
—Qiu Pu, 1983

LEFT   This Oroqen hunter uses a traditional bi-pod support of two sticks to hunt roe deer (*Capreolus capreolus*). Because hunting is now less prevalent than in the past, many Oroqen have turned to logging. In the past, Oroqen hunters set "ground arrows" fashioned like crossbows at specified locations along well-traveled paths. Any passing animal would trigger the firing mechanism. However, with the logging and increased traffic through the forests of the Hinggan Mountains, the Oroqen have been forced to abandon their native hunting techniques.

ABOVE   After a successful hunt, prepared skins of *paozi*, or roe deer, hang to dry.

*Any child of ten in Mongolia could fend for himself prudently and capably.
I have seen boys and girls of six or seven pick up a stick and dash out fearlessly
when they have sighted a wolf menacing the sheep herd—and have seen the wolf
slink away, frightened by the bold manner and voice of the child.*

—Frans August Larson, *1930*

ABOVE The Buriat Mongols I visited
live outside Hailar, in the Inner
Mongolian Autonomous Region.
With genuine Mongol hospitality,
this family of five Buriats—said to
be descended from Genghis Khan's
finest warriors—slaughtered a sheep
outside the *yurt* and held a mutton
feast in my honor. Aside from
sheep, the Mongols fry strips of
dough—a pastry called *bordzig*—
in oil made from melted chunks of
sheep fat. I was loath to refuse their
hospitality, which included having
to drink so much *kumiss*—fermented
mare's milk, the national drink of
Mongolia—that I had to cancel
scheduled meetings the next day!
The Buriat Mongol women prefer
to wear light brown dresses, pleated
below the waist to indicate their
married status. This extended family
lives in three *yurts* and collectively
owns more than 500 sheep. Mongol
yurts (round, felt tents), called *ger* in
the local language, are moved by ox
cart. The wooden lattice frame for
the *ger* consists of four to twelve
base walls, or *khana*, depending on
the size and wealth of the family.
A new *khana* is added for each new
family member.

Members of a 17th-century
mission from northeast China to
Tibet returned home as lamas, and
subsequently introduced the type
of Buddhism prevalent in Tibet
to the people of Mongolia and
Manchuria. Before that, Mongols
practiced shamanism.

The Mongols are a strong, hardy, and generally good-natured race... Every stranger is welcome, and has the best the host can give; the more he swallows of what is offered him, the better will be pleased the household... The staple dish of a Mongol yourt is boiled mutton, but it is unaccompanied with capers or any other kind of sauce or seasoning. A sheep goes to pot immediately on being killed, and the quantity that each man will consume is something surprising. When the meat is cooked it is lifted out of the hot water and handed, all dripping and steamy, to the guests. Each man takes a large lump on his lap, or any convenient support, and then cuts off little chunks which he tosses into his mouth as if it were a mill-hopper. The best piece is reserved for the guest of honor, who is expected to divide it with the rest; after the meat is devoured they drink the broth, and this concludes the meal. Knives and cups are the only aids to eating, and as every man carries his own "outfit," the Mongol dinner service is speedily arranged. The entire work consists in seating the party around a pot of cooked meat.

—Thomas W. Knox, 1873

ABOVE LEFT A Buriat Mongol woman holds her bundled seven-month old baby, with his head shaved in traditional style. In the past Mongols kept their infants in protective cradles at all times. Due to the relative inaccessibility of this remote region, the lack of basic medical care resulted in a high rate of infant mortality. However, the modernization of recent years has brought improved health care to the Mongols.

ABOVE RIGHT Mongol girl welcoming me to her family's home.

Bouriats, a people of Mongol descent who were conquered by Genghis Khan in the thirteenth century... cling to the manners of their race, and even when settled in villages are unwilling to live in houses. At the first of their villages after we passed the mountains I took opportunity to visit a yourt. It was a tent with a light frame of trellis work covered with thick felt, and I estimated its diameter at fifteen or eighteen feet. In the center the frame work has no covering, in order to give the smoke free passage. A fire, sometimes of wood and sometimes of dried cow-dung, burns in the middle of the yourt during the day and is covered up at night. I think the tent was not more than five and a half feet high...

—Thomas W. Knox, 1873

LEFT This Mongol herdsman drives his herd of sheep into a holding pen for the evening to guard against a wolf attack. Ferocious mastiffs protect the sheep all night and can repel most predators.

ABOVE Photographed in 1983, modern-day Mongols show off a new breed of horse: a jeep and motorcycle. While still clinging to their traditions as horsemen the Mongols have embraced many conveniences.

The herdsmen also break and train to the saddle all young animals. They generally select one or two of the speediest colts and train them in as lasso horses. For this only the most intelligent are selected, as the Mongol horseman demands that his mount work with him. The Mongolian lasso is a slender birch or willow pole about fifteen feet long, with a rope of rawhide at the end. The herdsman is too busy handling this implement to guide his horse. He rides without the use of his reins, and it is marvelous how quickly a lasso horse discovers which horse it is his rider desires to catch...

—*Frans August Larson, 1930*

As herdsmen, most of China's 4.8 million Mongol women and men are comfortable on horseback, and do little farming. During my visit, they demonstrated how to lasso an untrained horse. All Mongols wear boots with high heels, well suited to life in the saddle, and long robes to protect against the elements.

Living in the Huzhu Tu Autonomous County in Qinghai, the
192,600 Tu represent an interesting
cultural mix. Their language closely
resembles Mongolian, but Tu costumes and embroidery reflect a Han
influence, as do their agricultural
traditions. Yet like their Tibetan
neighbors, Tu women wear earrings
of silver, beads and tassels; they eat
large quantities of yak butter and
tsampa. During Tu festivals, a butter
sculpture—*torma*—representing

the earth, sun and moon sits over a
wooden bowl of *tsampa*—a reminder
of their days under the open sky,
eating *tsampa* and tending herds.
The Tu were nomads until 200
years ago.

Tu hospitality, which I encountered in the village of Dazhang,
mimics Mongolian traditions. Each
guest is required to drink three cups
of barley liquor. The host, meanwhile, sings a toast to the visitors.
Each round of three drinks is repeat-

ed thrice: before entering the
village, before entering the house
and prior to being seated.

Under the now-defunct Tu
practice of *daitiantou*, a Tu girl had to
be betrothed by her 18th birthday,
else her parents would "marry her
to heaven," forbidding a conven-
tional marriage. However, many
heaven-bound daughters still raised
families without a husband.

Sandwiched geographically and ethnically between Tibetans and Mongolians, 12,300 members of the Yugur nationality inhabit the northern range of the Qilian Mountains, in Gansu's Sunan Yugur Autonomous County. These 1991 pictures reveal traditional Yugur costumes worn during a wedding ceremony. Men and women both wear these characteristic, conical hats, usually made of felt, with red tassels; some wear the more modern-looking fedora. A blue silk robe with gold and red trim covers the left shoulder, with the right sleeve thrown off the shoulder in Tibetan style.

In a custom similar to that of the Mongols, families hold special hair-cutting ceremonies in late summer for Yugur girls at three years of age. Friends and relatives bring gifts for the lucky girl, who has survived beyond infancy, and have the honor of snipping off a lock of hair. Only after a special maturity ceremony at age 15 can she grow her hair long again, symbolizing her readiness for marriage.

XINJIANG
THE SILK ROAD

An ancient trade route stretching 6,440 km (4,000 mi) from the ancient Chinese capital of Chang'an (Xian) to the Roman Empire, the Silk Road influenced the rich history and culture of peoples living in the Xinjiang Uygur Autonomous Region. Xinjiang means "New Dominion" in Chinese, and at 1,709,400 sq km (660,000 sq mi) occupies one sixth of the country's land area. More than 15 million people live in Xinjiang, among them most of China's 7.2 million Uygurs. Other Islamic nationalities, such as Kazak, Kirgiz and Tajik, can also be found living in this sprawling and diverse region.

Bordered by Russia, Kazakstan, Kirgizstan, Tajikistan, Afghanistan, Pakistan, Kashmir, Tibet, Qinghai, Gansu and the Republic of Mongolia, Xinjiang is home to a distinctive mix of Turkic peoples. A few are employed in the industrial capital of Urumqi, while many others live by their traditional activities of farming and herding. Recently, Xinjiang's economy has been bolstered by the exploitation of oil deposits beneath the Taklamakan Desert.

Uygur civilization was built on an intricate system of underground wells and water channels that brings snowmelt down from the mountains to water the desert. In the counties of Turpan, Hami, Shanshan and Toksun, water flows from *karez*—ancient underground pipelines. The combination of hot summers and abundant water produces fine long-staple cotton, sweet grapes and prized Hami melons in the region.

Xinjiang was first brought under Chinese imperial control during the Qin dynasty (221–206 BC), and was subsequently conquered by the Uzbeks (seventh century), Tibetans (eighth century), Uygurs and Arabs (tenth century), Mongols (13th century) and Manchus (18th century). Xinjiang was declared a Chinese province in 1881, and later was reclassified as an autonomous region.

Behind the modern white houses, farther on towards the edge of the desert, we found a colony of Kazaks…living in their round igloo-like tents fashioned of a willow framework over which sheepskins and bits of carpet and felt are hung to keep out the weather. The roof is left open when a fire is burning inside the tent, and closing the roof is merely a matter of replacing the folded-back coverings… Light came from the bared framework of the roof. Strips of brightly coloured carpet and hand-woven rugs hung round the walls, over a layer of rush matting. On the floor there was a dark red carpet, and a number of brass kettles and jugs and wooden bowls. There was no furniture. In a scooped-out hollow in the middle of the floor a small fire of sticks and dried dung burned. A stolid thick-set woman with Mongolian features sat cross-legged on the carpet… [She] wore the long loose robe and white swathed head-dress of the Kazak women.

—Ethel Mannin, 1936

Kazak *yurts* rise like mushrooms from the plain at Lake Barkol. Perhaps Genghis Khan once rose from his tent and looked out on a scene like this.

PREVIOUS PAGE A Kazak man helps to assemble the *yurt's* frame.

After a dusty day of driving along the Tianshan Mountain Range in 1996, we came to a Kazak family erecting two new *yurts*—portable round houses with a willow framework, covered in layers of felt made from yak or sheep wool—which offer protection from climatic extremes. Kazak, Kirgiz, Mongols and Tajik use such houses. The *yurt's* greatest asset is its portability, accommodating nomadic peoples who travel seasonally to fresh grazing grounds. We watched in awe as nimble fingers assembled a ten-foot high structure in less than an hour.

"You must have a big family!" I said to the elder man. "My son Mulaqi is getting married tomorrow," beamed proud Kejier. The two new *yurts* would accommodate guests on the wedding day, the smaller one becoming Mulaqi and wife Pahtegul's new home as part of the *kalym*, or bride price. Colorful blankets, rugs, storage chests, a horse and several sheep rounded out the *kalym*.

China's 1.1 million Kazak raise sheep and goats—both called *yang* in Chinese—across a broad valley surrounding the shores of Lake Barkol ("the Lake of Leopards") in the Tianshan (Heavenly Mountain) Range. Goats can be distinguished from domestic sheep by their flat, pointed horns, straight coats and long, slit-shaped pupils. The animals are corraled for daily milking.

The first time I watched the milking process, I was shocked to see Kazak women punching the animals' udders. I later learned that this action imitated the nudging and prodding of their kids, stimulating milk flow. They were not taking out their aggression on the sheep after all!

Most nomadic Kazak families subsist wholly on a dairy and meat diet, as many herds number more than 500 animals. Sheep and goats only provide milk during the summer months. In contrast, the domestic yak of Tibetan nomads gives milk almost year round.

LEFT Although the railroad passes through Hami less than 100 km (62 mi) away, most nomads of Barkol Kazak Autonomous County resist the allure of modern conveniences. The Islamic Kazaks settled in Barkol after oppressive warlords in northern Xinjiang forced them to flee in the 1930s.

ABOVE Middle-aged Kazak women wrap their heads in colored scarves, or on festive occasions wear small, round caps of horsehide with owl feathers stuck in the middle. The older women wear embroidered white wimples, as seen here.

From the jutting shoulder the wings hang, their dark, shining plumes like an armour of overlapping plates. The heads of the birds are covered with leather hoods...The hooked beak is on a level with the man's forehead. The black talons are enormous, and issue from a grey, scaly sheath of skin to grasp the leather glove which, in order that the reins may be held, is cut for only one finger and a thumb. The bird tries to tear a piece off with its beak. A slip-knot fastens a long thong to one foot. The man's fist rests on a wooden fork socketed in the saddle.

　　The nape of the eagle's neck is a tuft of white disordered feathers. The hood removed, the implacable eye appears, glittering like a jewel.

—Ella Maillart, 1935

PREVIOUS PAGES While horses and camels are still used widely in Barkol, some young Kazaks find motorcycles more their speed. The wedding *yurts* stand completed in the background.

The bond between man and hunting eagle lasts for life, with the bird's name a well-kept secret. Mulidebke, this proud, 65 year-old Kazak hunter of Lake Barkol, refused to reveal the name of his prized eagle of 13 years, fearing we might call him away. He captured this golden eagle as a chick. Such birds are initially treated with deliberate cruelty, forced to perch on a thin string, wearing a hood, for ten days. Gradually, the eagle learns to trust its master and is rewarded with small branches, and finally a comfortably large perch.

Hunters ride out with eagles in winter; a special, forked stick in the saddle supports the weight of the bird. Foxes are the main prey, and provide fur for the traditional Kazak hat. Three layers of thick camel hide in the leather glove protect Mulidebke's hand from the piercing grip of his eagle's talons.

I was happy to learn that 11 of 80 Kazak households in Barkol—nearly 14 percent—still raised hunting eagles in 1996. Kirgiz and Naxi men still practice falconry as well. Like the Kazak, Kirgiz use golden eagles and Saker falcons. The Naxi use a smaller hunting eagle to catch up to 200 pheasants and hares each year, traditionally meeting on the 15th day of the eighth moon to buy and sell birds.

Kazak Nomads on the move, then and now. Several domestic, double-humped Bactrian camels (*Camelus bactrianus*) can move a medium-sized *yurt* from one campsite to another, but a single jeep proves to be more efficient. At the Khartan Valley in Aksai Kazak Autonomous County, this means three days of plodding versus just three hours on a bumpy road. With his 19-year-old son translating, Kazak elder Silam Mubai revealed that he paid 20,000 yuan (US$2,400) in 1996 for the second-hand Beijing Jeep—twice the family's yearly household income. The family still raises camels, however, to navigate sand dunes, which jeeps cannot penetrate.

It is really marvelous with what rapidity and ease the Chinese servants free their camels of our loads. One after another, as they arrive, the various sections are led forward, the animals made to lie down, the poles drawn out of the two loops... Both boxes are on the ground, ready, next morning, after another manipulation just as simple, to occupy again their former position on the back of the camel.

—Sven Hedin, 1931

In 1982, A Kazak family in Golmud packs camp in preparation for a move—typical in the life of a nomad. Visible are the folding willow sections of the *yurt*, red wall hangings for the interior, and the kitchen's chimney and stove.

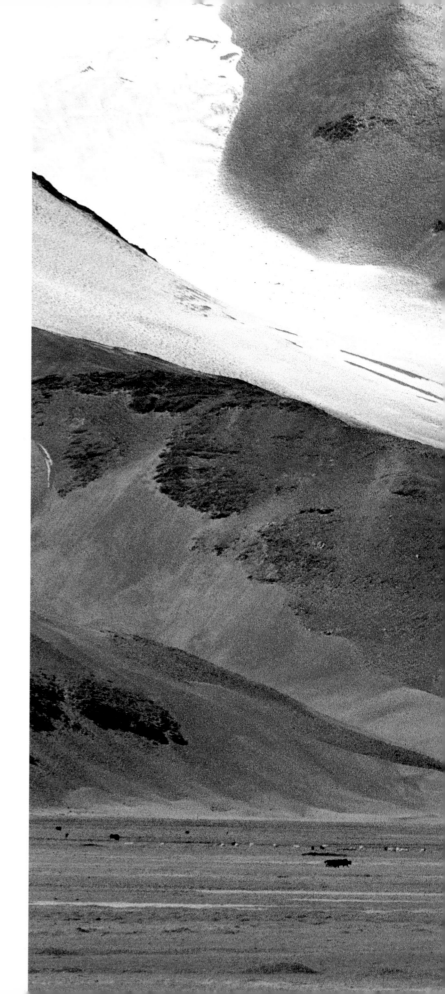

As we rode across a wide grassy plain towards a group of akhois, the native dwellings that look like huge bee-hives, it was the hour of the afternoon milking, and the Kirghiz women in gaily coloured coats, long leather boots and the characteristic lofty white headgear, were busily at work. They had tied the sheep and the goats and the black, brown or parti-coloured yaks to long ropes and let the animals go free one by one when they had been milked, a loud chorus of bleating and grunting going on all the time.

—*Ella Sykes*, 1920

Kirgiz *yurts* dot the landscape near the Pamirs, where China borders Tajikistan, Afghanistan, Pakistan and India. A fresh dusting of snow at 4,000 meters (13,123 ft) complements the scene.

... the fight for the goat's carcass began... The object was to reach the carcass from the saddle and ride away with it. It was a most fantastic fracas. All of the eighty riders crowded together. Some horses reared, others fell. Riders were thrown, and had to find their way out of the melee to avoid being crushed to death. From the edge of the circle, other Kirghiz pressed forward, worming their horses in among the others...

—Sven Hedin, 1925

During a rough and tumble, the Kirgiz engage in *baigu*, a national pastime in which horseback riders play tug-of-war with a decapitated goat, the victor being he who carries it across the goal line. Like other steppe nomads, the Kirgiz also enjoy wrestling and all forms of horseback competition.

The hunting eagle is captured by means of a live fox tied to a rope... When captured the unfortunate bird is confined to a dark room, its eyelids are sewn up, and its spirit is broken by the incessant beating of drums which allows it no sleep. It remains morose for a time, refusing all food, but gradually becomes tame and attaches itself to the man who feeds it and takes it out hunting.

—Ella Sykes, 1920

Ready to take flight on a hunting expedition, a well-trained falcon perches on the arm of a Kirgiz horseman from Sumatashi, near Akqi, western Xinjiang in 1984. For two months every year, starting in October, groups of Kirgiz men set out with their trained eagles and falcons, to hunt for prey such as rabbit, pika, fox and gazelle. The falconer wears a *kalpak*, a traditional white pointed hat trisected with black trim.

The Kirghiz… lead a free and varied life moving with their great herds of sheep, goats, yaks and camels from pasture to pasture (usually within the same valley basin), according to the seasons. They make occasional journeys to the oases of the plains to trade their sheep, skins and butter for flour, salt and other needs. Like all nomads of Central Asia, they are splendid horsemen, for, of course, riding is an indispensable part of their lives… There is, I suppose, a tendency to over-idyllize the simple life; but if contentment, physical well-being and a means of livelihood which tends to promote individual dignity and self-reliance together constitute a yardstick by which to measure a standard of living, then, certainly, that of the Kirghiz is high in relation to the majority of human beings.

—Eric Shipton, 1951

Even when tending livestock, Kirgiz women dress impeccably in their national costume. Kirgiz men, on the other hand, opt for the western clothes of modern China. One of ten Islamic groups in the country, the 143,500 Kirgiz mainly inhabit Akqi, in Xinjiang's Kizilsu Kirgiz Autonomous Prefecture, along the Kirgizstan border. Although some Kirgiz still maintain their traditional pastoral lifestyle, many have settled into a more agricultural life.

Unmarried Kirgiz girls braid their hair in six to eight plaits, wearing a round wool cap over the top. Married women wear a white headscarf over two braids, which they adorn with silver ornaments. They also wear silver bracelets and rings, and affix silver buttons to their intricately designed vests. Among the Kirgiz, both men and women are excellent horsemen. A Xinjiang proverb says, "The eagle has his wings—the man, his horse."

"Akoi" is a Turki word (it means literally "white house") for the dome-shaped tent used by all the nomads of Turkestan and Mongolia. It consists of a light, skeleton frame of wood, covered with a jacket of felt...Normally they have a floor diameter of about fifteen feet and are about nine feet high. The richer ones are decorated with gaily embroidered felts. The fire is laid on the centre of the floor, and there is a hole in the apex of the tent through which the smoke (most of it) escapes...It is a very comfortable form of dwelling; there is no draught and even in the coldest weather it is pleasantly warm inside. It can be assembled or taken down in about an hour and can be carried by one camel or two ponies.

—Eric Shipton, 1951

ABOVE The Kirgiz in the Chinese Pamirs live in *akhoi*—a collapsible felt tent, similar to the Kazak yurt. Five or six sections of *khana*, a folding, lattice framework of willow, give the structure its shape. Several pieces of woolen felt cover the yurt. Highly practical for the nomadic Kirgiz, *akhoi* are not scrapped and replaced wholesale; each section is replaced as needed—the willow frame, the felt covering, the door, the woven strips that bind it together. Decorations on the *akhoi* indicate status of a family. This particular group lives west of Muztagata in the Pamirs, their grazing area during the summer months.

OPPOSITE PAGE A Kirgiz family relaxes in an *akhoi* near Subashi (Head of the Waters), in the Chinese Pamirs, just north of Kuqa. The stringed instrument the child plays generally accompanies recitation of the longest Kirgiz literary work, the Manaxi, consisting of 200,000 verses.

Taxkorgan serves as the government seat of the Tajik Autonomous County in western Xinjiang. Just north of here, Muztagata—"the Father of Ice Mountains"—boasts a spectacular ice-covered summit at 7,546 meters (24,757 ft). According to Sven Hedin, the Kirgiz believe Mount Muztagata to be the tomb of a giant saint, where the bodies of Moses and Ali rest. Legend also holds that a utopian city called Janaidar lay atop the peak—a place with no cold, no suffering and no death.

In describing the Pamirs, Marco Polo supposed "the surrounding summits to be the highest lands in the world," and suggested that weakened livestock would be fattened in just ten days by grazing in the lush pastures. These days local herdsman do exactly that, keeping sheep, goats, horses and camels.

In the monotonous, dull-yellow landscape, in which here and there the earth reflects a faint green light with the young grass of summer and of isolated hills of the steppe, but occasionally is almost entirely bare, the long, winding caravan affords a majestic, overpowering prospect. The foremost camels, which are almost lost to sight in the distance, show up like a string of fine black beads; those immediately following are swinging along at a steady pace with their heavy burdens. On either side ride the soldiers, chatting and singing. When I turn round I can scarcely see the end of the mighty procession, which fills the whole landscape. The camels are not heard at all. Their light steps make no sound in the soft, dusty soil, like those of a cat. The only sounds that one hears are the creaking of the wooden boxes rubbing against the poles of the pack-saddles, the jarring and rattling of the handles and locks on the iron-protected chests, the screaming of a camel that has broken loose... and the rush of the north wind.

—Sven Hedin, 1931

Two camels belonging to members of the Tajik nationality trek through a riverbed in the Pamirs along the Karakoram Highway. The way west through the Wakhan Corridor into Afghanistan is one of many routes along the Silk Road. More recently, the highway across the Kunjirap Pass to Pakistan has revived trade and eclipsed the old footpaths.

ABOVE Historically, merchants crossed the Pamirs as they traveled along the ancient Silk Road. The Tajik, who speak a form of Persian, live in the Chinese Pamirs, bordering Pakistan. Tajik are the only Shiite Muslims in China, the other nine groups being Sunni. Traditionally nomadic herders, many Tajik have now settled into a sedentary lifestyle. Most Tajik women wear round, embroidered hats with a scarf suspended from the back. Silver earrings and elaborate beadwork adorn the head of this married woman. Brides wear a red shawl at their wedding to symbolize happiness.

OPPOSITE PAGE Friends and relatives, dressed in their finest garments, gather at the bride's home, as dancing and feasting continues throughout the entire evening. Two men play flutes to accompany drums played by women. Such flutes, fashioned from a single eagle's shoulder bones and played in tandem, demonstrate the importance of the eagle to the Tajik. The Tajik groom dances with his arms akimbo, simulating the outspread wings of eagles in flight. Members of the same sex often perform such dances in pairs.

The Pamirs are a series of valleys connected with an extensive mountain system in which centuries of glacial action, together with the effects of wind and weather, have gradually worn down the mountain spurs and filled up the intervening valleys…until a series of comparatively flat plains alternate with rugged snow-covered peaks and glacier-bound ridges. The word Pamir signifies desert. It is derived from the Khokandese. The great elevation at which the Pamirs lie…has given rise to the term "roof of the world," which is generally applied to the region by picturesque writers.

—Ralph P. Cobbold, 1900

ABOVE Tajik women gather inside a yurt, separate from the men, at a friend's wedding in 1984.

RIGHT This married Tajik woman of the Pamirs wears the white veil of Islam. The Tajik are the only group of Shiite Muslims within China.

In a wedding procession in the Pamirs, this Tajik groom wears a turban of intertwined red and white scarves. His shoulders are later sprinkled with white flour for good luck. Tajik weddings are three-day festivals. On the second day, before the bride leaves her parental home, much of the celebration of dancing, singing and feasting focuses around the hearth. The bride wears a long white veil, a red scarf and strings of buttons braided on her long hair, as a symbol of her readiness for marriage.

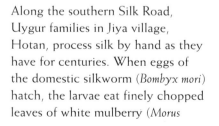

Along the southern Silk Road, Uygur families in Jiya village, Hotan, process silk by hand as they have for centuries. When eggs of the domestic silkworm (*Bombyx mori*) hatch, the larvae eat finely chopped leaves of white mulberry (*Morus alba*) for 35 days, at which point the worms spin cocoons. Some pupae are saved for breeding, but most are boiled or steamed in their cocoons to loosen the sericin, a gelatinous protein that binds the silken threads together.

Stirring silkworm cocoons, Uygur women, wearing silk dresses in traditional patterns, reel raw silk onto a hand-cranked wooden wheel. The silk strands are then thrown, twisted and doubled to vary the strength and thickness. Uygur artisans then dye or bleach the silk and weave it into a variety of fabrics. Although mechanized weaving takes place, the finest silk is still woven by hand. One local family still makes paper by hand, from the pulp of mulberry bark, as a by-product of silk production.

It is said that feeding the leaves of 30 mulberry trees to silkworms produces just three kilograms (6.6 lb) of silk. A strand of silk from one worm alone can stretch as far as 46 meters (151 ft).

Clays, marls, sandstone and limestone prevail on the outer border of the Altyn-tagh, porphory is not uncommon in the higher parts, but granite is rare. Water is very deficient in these mountains, even springs are rare, and in such as are to be met with, the water is mostly of a bitter-saline flavour. These hills are in general characterized by extreme sterility, the scanty vegetation being confined to the upper valleys and gorges...

—Nikolai Prejevalsky, 1879

At the Arjin Shan (Altun Mountain) Nature Reserve in the Xinjiang Uygur Autonomous Region, a group of Uygur nomads move their belongings to autumn camp at Khartan, the Black Hills, via camel caravan. This reserve, managed by the National Environmental Protection Agency, was largely devoid of human habitation until the central government established the 44,872 sq km (17,325 sq mi) reserve in May, 1983. At that point, local administrators of nearby Nanshan district in Ruoqiang County, Bayingolin Mongolian Autonomous Prefecture, moved 30 Uygur families onto the land with 170,000 head of sheep. Due to the harsh conditions of life in Arjin Reserve, only 13 families—fewer than 100 people—and 8,000 sheep remained in 1997.

In the middle of the march the track led us out of the salt-flats into a strange country of small dunes and twisted tamarisk. There was something forced and unnatural about the landscape. The little hummocks, the naked branches, looked—against the too bright, too picturesque background of sky and mountains—like the synthetic scenery which surrounds stuffed wild animals in a glass case. The snow and the mosquitoes, the dry hollow contrasting with the bog on top of the ridge beyond it—everything seemed freakish and abnormal.

—*Peter Fleming, 1936*

LEFT Parched earth lines the road-side in the little oil town of Huatugou, en route to the Arjin Shan Reserve from Dunhuang.

ABOVE Snow-covered sand dunes rise to 4,000 meters (13,123 ft) in the Arjin Mountain Nature Reserve, just beyond the Uygur settlement of Tufangzi. Aridity reigns across the plateau, making such precipitation a rare and welcome sight. Below the sand dunes, wild yak roam in pasturelands watered by an extensive freshwater marsh—also home to the rare black-necked crane.

I sat down calmly on the bank, and felt my pulse. It was so weak that it was hardly noticeable—only forty-nine beats. Then I drank, and drank again. I drank without restraint. The water was cold, clear as crystal, and as sweet as the best spring-water. And then I drank again. My dried-up body absorbed the moisture like a sponge. All my joints softened, all my movements became easier. My skin, hard as parchment before, now became softened. My forehead grew moist. The pulse increased in strength; and after a few minutes it was fifty-six. The blood flowed more freely in my veins. I had a feeling of well-being and comfort. I drank again, and sat caressing the water in this blessed pool. Later on, I christened this pool Khoda-verdi-kol, or "The Pool of God's Gift."

—*Sven Hedin, 1925*

This Uygur family drives their herd of sheep and goats to the last well at desert's edge for one month a year. They eke out a precarious existence here, drinking bitter water from a mineral-filled well. The *huyangshu* tree, literally "foreign poplar," indicates a subterranean water supply. The family's son, not pictured here, became my guide into the desert to help search for an ancient fortress in 1993.

This remote well lies north of Qiemo, in southern Xinjiang, at the southern edge of the Taklamakan Desert—at 518,000 sq km (200,000 sq mi) the largest desert in China. In Turkic, Taklamakan means "go in and do not come out." Beyond this well lies a stretch of waterless desert that takes camel-borne travellers 40 days to cross.

Swedish explorer Sven Hedin gives a gruesome account of his six days in the Taklamakan without water, in which most of his men and his faithful dog Yoldash perished. To quench their thirst, the desperate men had tried unsuccessfully to drink the spirits used to power the stove, coagulated sheep's blood and camel urine. Fortunately, Hedin finally reached a small pool of water. He hoped to carry some of the precious liquid to his companion, but was at a loss for a proper container. Finally, he hit upon a solution—his waterproof boots!

LEFT This Uygur man, characterized by his square hat with fine embroidery, commutes between two homes: one a remote outpost in Tufangzi, at 3,700 meters (12,139 ft), in the Arjin Shan Reserve; the other a town dwelling in Ruoqiang, Xinjiang. The reserve's harsh environment, many salt-water lakes and an average elevation of 4,500 meters (14,764 ft) make life here a constant challenge. Yexiekpati Lake is the lowest point in the reserve, at 3,876 meters (12,717 ft). Like other Uygurs in Tufangzi, this man raises sheep. Most Uygurs, however, live in settled agricultural communities.

China's 7.2 million Uygurs speak a Turkic language and live mainly in southern Xinjiang. Devout Muslims, like many other groups in Xinjiang, their language is closely related to Kirgiz, Kazak and Mongolian.

OPPOSITE PAGE In remote Da Mazar—Big Mausoleum—in southern Xinjiang, a Uygur family guards the tomb of Isaca, an Islamic sage who died more than 200 years ago. Despite their difficult existence, these two Uygur girls take great pride in the family's work. Old fragments of the Koran have been found in this historic desert area.

OPPOSITE PAGE Symbolic of the remoteness and vastness of the Arjin Reserve, a Uygur man rides camelback near the village of Tufangzi.

ABOVE This Uygur family, with their mule cart, just moved to Tufangzi (Mud Houses). The town once served as a staging ground for hunting expeditions when domestic food supplies failed.

FAUNA
FLORA

China is home to 1.2 billion people concentrated in its central and coastal regions. As shown in previous sections, however, the nation's minorities tend to live along the borders, especially to the north and west. Because of the harsh environment there, human settlements are widely scattered and the effects of modernization limited. As a result, natural spaces in this, China's "Wild West," still exist, allowing a unique variety of plant, bird and mammal life to flourish. Few people envision such natural wonders when they think of the recent growth and development in coastal and central China.

In western China's uplands, for instance, alpine flowers have adapted to the harsh environment. Roughly 900 species of the genus *Rhododendron* have been identified worldwide, with at least 460 recorded in China, and over 270 species on the Tibetan Plateau alone. Large ungulate (hoofed mammal) populations roam across the plateau, including the rugged wild yak, Tibetan antelope, playful *kiang* (wild ass) and elusive wild Bactrian camels.

The establishment of wildlife protection areas, including the Changtang Reserve in northern Tibet and the Arjin Shan Nature Reserve in southeastern Xinjiang—China's two largest—displays a concern for the future of the plateau's spectacular fauna and flora. However, only with the diligent enforcement of wildlife protection laws will these vast areas be preserved for future generations.

[Tibetan antelope] are graceful animals, about the size of the American pronghuck which used to live on the plains of our West in millions. They are fawn-colored, dark on the back and almost white on the belly. The male has beautiful tapering horns, sometimes in the shape of a lyre. How they lived in this barren country was a source of constant wonder to us. Their only food seemed to be the sparse tufts of dried grass that were scattered over the surrounding country at very infrequent intervals. They seemed to thrive on this meager diet, as those we killed were as fat as butter-balls.

—*Theodore and Kermit Roosevelt, 1926*

Tibetan antelope (*Pantholops hodgsoni*) prefer flat, terrain 4,000 to 5,000 meters (13,123–16,404 ft) in elevation, and range over 800,000 sq km (308,880 sq mi) of the Tibetan Plateau. Herds usually number fewer than 25, though larger groups occur in November in preparation for the rut. Schaller has seen as many as 350 animals group together, while C. Rawling reported herds of 15,000 to 20,000 in 1905. Like the wild ass, the Tibetan antelope— known locally as *chiru*, or *orongo* in Mongolian—has a well-developed heart as big as that of an ox, which explains its ability to sprint effortlessly across the plain at such high altitudes. The male *chiru's* graceful, notched horns reach nearly 0.6 meters (2 ft) into the air; females lack horns. Here several male antelope make their way across the Arjin Shan Nature Reserve in late September.

PREVIOUS PAGE A herd of wild asses.

The summer colour of the head and back is grey (in winter light fawn with a grizzly tinge); under-parts, white; on the buttocks the white area forms a large, conspicuous patch; tip of tail, black. The male has black horns, nearly erect for a short distance, then curving sharply backwards...A full-grown Goa stands about 24 inches high at shoulder; the flesh is said to be good eating.

—*Ernest Henry Wilson, 1913*

The most widespread of the plateau's grassland ungulates (hoofed mammals), Tibetan gazelle (*Procapra picticaudata*) gather in small herds of up to a dozen animals. Known to the Chinese as *bai pigu* for the conspicuous patch of white on their rump, they can sprint at 60 km (37 mi) per hour. Called *goa* by Tibetans, male gazelle sport small horns; females have none.

[Wild asses] were on this and many later stages of our route the only decoration of a naked landscape. They were a good decoration too. The size of a mule, dark brown in colour with pale bellies, they wheeled and galloped in the middle distance with heads up and short tails flying. They ranged in herds of anything up to fifteen, and in their manoeuvres achieved that uncanny unanimity of movement which you see sometimes in a covey of partridges or a flock of teal; no troop of cavalry was ever more symmetrically ranked, more precisely simultaneous in its evolutions... They are very attractive animals to watch.

—Peter Fleming, 1936

A trio of wild asses sprints across the plains of western Tibet.

The adult animal stands about a yard tall at the withers and has a long, narrow head, short ears, no mane or beard, and a thick, close coat of hair. The general colour of the upper-parts is brownish-grey tinged with slaty-blue, darker in summer than in winter; under-parts white; lower part of tail black…The horns are blackish-olive with an S-like curvature, rounded and nearly smooth save for the annual ring of growth. The horns of the ewes are short, drawn together at the base, curving upwards and outwards in somewhat scimitar-like fashion.

—Ernest Henry Wilson, 1913

ABOVE A young blue sheep in Aksai County rested six meters (20 ft) away as I approached. It repeatedly stood up and lay down, nervous but unsure how to react to human presence. It finally fled over the ridge to join its herd.

RIGHT A herd of *bharal*, or blue sheep (*Pseudois nayaur*), in the Khartan area of the Arjin Shan Reserve. One ram leads while another brings up the rear. Blue sheep prefer steep, difficult cliff country. The blue sheep's name derives from its summer coat, tinged bluish-grey.

ABOVE Though Tibetans have raised white-lipped deer (*Cervus albirostris*) for centuries, the state-run Tola Deer Farm, on the northern edge of the Tibetan Plateau, was established only ten years ago. Here about twenty Tibetan, Muslim and Han families manage some 200 white-lipped deer and 400 wapiti. After the bucks' antlers are harvested in late June, they are sold for use in traditional Chinese medicine for 8,000 yuan (US$966) per kilogram. The entire farm yielded 200 kg (441 lb) of antlers in 1996.

OPPOSITE PAGE Because argali "bighorn" sheep (*Ovis ammon*) inhabit inaccessible mountains of northwest China, it is more common to find argali skulls than live animals. Trophy hunting, regulated by the Chinese government, brings in up to US$15,000 a head for argali, called *nyan* in Tibetan.

I believe that the bighorn, or argali, as the Mongols call it, holds the first place of all non-dangerous game as a sportsman's trophy... [He] holds his head with its great circlet of horns as proudly as if he were a Roman warrior and, even when running away, he never looks undignified.

—*Roy Chapman Andrews, 1924*

We had stooped on the very edge of the ice sheet, and on the far side of it the men soon perceived a black object, which they took to be a stone. But it moved... "There's a bear! It's making straight for the camp!" And, sure enough, Bruin, not taking the slightest notice of either the tents or the camels, was marching calmly towards us as though he belonged to us...

Bruin came on again, marching straight to his doom. The three shots rang out as though they were one. Bruin did not stop, but went off at a gallop up the slope past the camp... Another volley and down tumbled the brute, rolling like a ball to the bottom of the steep declivity... His teeth showed that he was an ancient male, for they were full of gaping, big holes. He must have suffered horribly from toothache, but it was now radically cured. In his stomach we found a marmot, which he had just devoured, and several herbs. The former he had swallowed whole, skin and all, although he had been unable to crush its bones.

—Sven Hedin, 1903

A brown bear (*Ursus arctos*) ambles away from our vehicle in the Arjin Shan Nature Reserve.

The desert is not altogether a desert; it has a great deal of sand and general desolation to the day's ride, but is far from being a forsaken region where a wolf could not make a living. Antelopes abound, and are often seen in large droves as upon our Western plains... there are wild geese, ducks, and curlew in the ponds and... all in all, the country might be much worse than it is—which is bad enough.

—Thomas W. Knox, 1873

I spotted this wolf (*Canis lupus*) near the headwaters of the Yangtze, just north of Yushu (Jyekundo). Wolves are widespread predators of the plateau, found as high as 5,300 meters (17,388 ft) above sea level. Pastoralists have little tolerance for the creature and will shoot it on sight. Unlike other plateau animals, wolves receive no legal protection.

ABOVE LEFT This fox in Aksai County is probably a Tibetan fox (*Vulpes ferrilata*), although red fox (*Vulpes vulpes*) are found in the area as well.

ABOVE RIGHT A weasel (*Mustela eversmanni*) standing up to survey his surroundings near Serxu, Sichuan, displays a thick winter coat.

OPPOSITE PAGE LEFT Himalayan marmots (*Marmota himalayana*), in yellow summer coats, inhabit the Tibetan Plateau at elevations up to 5,000 meters (16,404 ft). Although some Tibetans hunt marmots for their lush fur, they rarely eat the meat.

OPPOSITE PAGE RIGHT Several species of pika (*Ochotona* sp.) occur on the Tibetan Plateau up to the vegetation line. Living in shallow burrows, pikas forage several hours a day, providing a ready food supply for predators such as bears and raptors. Hume's ground jays and snow finches readily nest in pika burrows on the treeless plateau.

The real owners of the soil, or rather the sub-soil, are the marmots. The are found in great masses on the plateaux, and their holes are dangerous stumbling-blocks for our horses. You see them scattered about everywhere, often in pairs, sitting upright on their bottoms, like gossiping housewives. I believe that they actually are gossiping, because they sit face to face and keep tapping each other with their forepaws, uttering little cries...

—Andre Guibaut, 1948

ABOVE A Tibetan man plays with his pet lynx (*Felis lynx*) at Manigango, Sichuan.

RIGHT En route to the Yangtze headwaters in 1985, my Tibetan guide Guodor shot this Tibetan antelope (*Pantholops hodgsoni*), or *chiru*, for food. Despite the creature's protected status, enforcement is difficult in these remote parts; here we had been riding on horseback for several days.

Chiru face grave threats from poachers, who kill them by the thousands for their fine, woolen undercoats. Antelope wool, called *shahtoosh*, "the king of wool," has become a big money-earner on the Tibetan Plateau. Woven *shahtoosh* scarfs retail for US$3,000–8,000 in London, Paris and New York. Three *chiru* are killed for every *shahtoosh* shawl produced; thus the fashion

industry is responsible for tens of thousands of animal deaths. In the winter of 1992 alone, staff at Xinjiang's Arjin Shan Reserve confiscated more than 2,000 antelope skins.

This raw wool is first shipped to Lhasa then smuggled to Nepal, where skins can fetch up to US$100. In 1992, Indian authorities confiscated the wool of more than 13,000 Tibetan antelope. The Forestry Bureau estimates that only 58,000 *chiru* remain in Tibet, while antelope expert George Schaller puts the world-wide figure at 75,000. Herds as large as 20,000 roamed the Tibetan Plateau less than a century ago. Until the demand for *shahtoosh* in the world's fashion markets diminishes, the *chiru* will continue their plummet towards extinction.

OPPOSITE PAGE This man displays feathers in a dazzling array of rainbow colors with pure white—the remains of Class Two-protected Lady Amherst's pheasants (*Chrysolophus amherstiae*). He sells each of the six skins for a mere US$1.45.

ABOVE LEFT A young man hawks a Himalayan snowcock (*Tetrogallus himalayensis*) at the roadside in the Chinese Pamirs.

ABOVE RIGHT A teenage boy sells this ring-necked pheasant (*Phasianus colchicus*)—one of more than 19 subspecies in China—along the roadside near Dengchuan, 60 km (37 mi) south of Lijiang, Yunnan province. He had bought the bird for the equivalent of US$3.60 and sought to double the price. The fact that such sales are illegal does little to deter enterpreneurs.

LEFT Widespread across the Tibetan Plateau up to 4,600 meters (15,092 ft), the bar-headed goose (*Anser indicus*) is so named for two striking black bars on the back of its white head.

ABOVE Tibetan sandgrouse (*Syrraptes tibetanus*) hide nests on the ground, where the young remain until they are able to fly. The birds breed at heights of up to 5,500 meters (18,045 ft), rarely venturing below 4,000 meters (13,123 ft).

ABOVE The Himalayan griffon (*Gyps himalayensis*) is a ubiquitous scavenger of the Tibetan Plateau. After gorging itself on a carcass, such vultures may be grounded for hours.

OPPOSITE PAGE The image of the crane graces many aspects of Chinese life, from motifs at the Imperial Palace in Beijing to New Year's posters on a peasant's wall. Poets have long praised the crane's elegant form; painters depict its graceful movements with fine brushstrokes. An important part of Chinese culture, the crane has come to represent longevity and prosperity, its courtship and pairing activities symbolizing a long and stable relationship.

In 1994 I initiated a conservation project for the rare black-necked crane (*Grus nigricollis*), managed by the China Exploration and Research Society. It seeks to educate village schoolchildren and farmers of Xundian County, Yunnan, about protecting the black-necked crane. The project also gives farmers economic aid, since the wintering birds pillage cash crops.

ABOVE Previously spread over much of northeastern China, the range of the red-crowned crane (*Grus japonensis*) has greatly diminished. The species still breeds at Zhalong Nature Reserve, one of China's first wildlife sanctuaries, just southeast of Qiqihar, in Heilongjiang province.

RIGHT Of 15 species of crane in the world, eight live in China. The

black-necked crane is the only one to spend its entire life high on the Tibetan Plateau. The birds breed and nest at an elevation of 4,000 to 4,500 meters (13,123–14,764 ft) as far north as the Qilian Mountains, and winter in Yunnan, Guizhou, and the Lhasa River valley. Experts believe 5,500 black-necked cranes remain in the wild.

ABOVE Yellow and pink betony (*Pedicularis* sp.) grow from 2,700 to 5,300 meters (8,858–17,388 ft) in marshy areas of Tibet, northwestern Yunnan and western Sichuan. The entire plant is said to help invigorate the spleen.

LEFT Because strong ultraviolet rays can damage cell chromosomes, the petals of alpine plants have developed their own protection. The more exposure petals get, the more carotene and anthocyanin they produce. Both draw the sun's rays away from cell chromosomes, thereby protecting the plant. Carotene deepens yellow tones in plants, while anthocyanin enhances the reds, blues and purples in a flower. This partially explains why wild alpine plants replanted to gardens at lower altitudes never seem quite as vivid as in their natural environment.

RIGHT The yellow poppy (*Meconopsis integrifolia*), whose flower can grow to more than eight inches across, thrives among bushes, slopes or meadows at altitudes of 3,500 to 5,000 meters (11,483–16,404 ft), adding a welcome splash of color to high mountain passes on the Tibetan Plateau. Doctors of Tibetan medicine prescribe yellow poppies to cure coughs and lower fever, while lamas collect poppies to make yellow dye. Among the yellow poppy's fans is Ernest Henry Wilson, a pioneering naturalist in western China who described it as "quite possibly the most gorgeous plant extant." I use the poppy as an altimeter on mountain passes.

FOLLOWING PAGE, CLOCKWISE FROM TOP LEFT
The Asiatic blue poppy (*Meconopsis horridula*) grows in rocky crevices and mountain slopes upwards of 4,000 meters (13,123 ft) in western Sichuan, Gansu, Qinghai and Tibet. Those growing at higher elevations have shorter stems to conserve energy. The blue poppy is used in Tibetan medicine to treat carbuncles, hepatitis and hypertension.

A species of rhubarb (*Rheum* sp.), or *da huang*, grows along rocky waterways above 4,200 meters (13,780 ft). Early this century, E. H. Wilson described its "broad, rounded, decurved, pale yellow bracts overlapping one another like tiles on a house roof," which turn red in late autumn. Said to cure constipation and dysentery, yellow rhubarb is sometimes cultivated in Chinese gardens.

Blue larkspur (*Delphinium* sp.) grows high on the Tibetan Plateau.

Over 900 species of rhododendron have been identified worldwide, with more than 460 species identified in China. Of those, roughly 270 grow on the Tibetan Plateau. Their colors range from scarlet and purple to white and yellow. Although some rhododendrons grow at sea level, most flourish at elevations of 2,500 to 4,600 meters (8,202–15,092 ft). This particular rhododendron graced an old growth forest just 100 meters below Daxue Shankou, a mountain pass through sheer granite cliffs.

Throughout all the mountainous parts...the most excellent kind of rhubarb is pro-
duced, in large quantities, and the merchants who come to buy it convey it to all
parts of the world. It is a fact that when they take that road, they cannot venture
amongst the mountains with any beasts other than those accustomed to the coun-
try, on account of a poisonous plant growing there, which, if eaten by them, has
the effect of causing the hoofs of the animals to drop off. Those of the country,
however, being aware of its dangerous quality, take care to avoid it.

—Marco Polo, on the dangers of wild rhubarb to livestock

CLOCKWISE FROM TOP LEFT This bold, purple iris (*Iris bulleyana*), endemic to Tibet, Yunnan and Sichuan, grows in damp meadows, on grassy slopes and in coniferous forests, from 2,300 to 4,800 meters (7,546–15,748 ft).

Trumpet flowers (*Incarvillea* sp.) grow along the roadside in high mountain passes of northern Yunnan and western Sichuan. Its roots are used to treat dizziness and anemia, lower blood pressure and regulate menstruation.

A common roadside plant found on grassy slopes and alluvial areas, starwort (*Stellera chamaejasme*) grows at altitudes of 3,500 to 4,600 meters (11,483–15,092 ft). Aside from killing parasitic worms, the roots cure dropsy, scabies and heart disease. Also said to be effective against a variety of cancers, starwort fibers can be used in making paper.

Yellow poppy in full bloom, high on a mountain pass.

TIBETAN PLATEAU

Situated between the Kunlun Mountains in the north and Himalayas to the south, the vast, arid Tibetan Plateau extends beyond Tibet Autonomous Region into parts of Xinjiang, Qinghai, Gansu, Sichuan, Yunnan, India, Bhutan, Nepal and Myanmar. Generous estimates place the size of this vast plateau at 2.3 million sq km (888,030 sq mi); the Tibet Autonomous Region itself is only 1,221,700 sq km (471,700 sq mi). Many of Asia's great rivers—the Yangtze, Yellow, Salween, Mekong and Brahmaputra (Yarlung Tsangpo) originate on the Tibetan Plateau.

The estimated 2.2 million people of the plateau, who are largely Tibetan, sustain themselves by raising yaks and sheep. They also practice agriculture, with highland barley a staple crop. Other ethnic peoples of this region include the Lhoba and Tu. Tibet's capital at Lhasa is the worldwide center of a form of Buddhism that developed in Tibet after the introduction of Indian Buddhism in the seventh century.

Six years after the 1959 declaration of Communist rule on the plateau, Tibet was named an autonomous region. After suffering severe economic and cultural setbacks during the Cultural Revolution, China's policy in Tibet has been aimed at development within the framework of traditional culture. Yet modernization has been slow to reach most parts of the rugged and inaccessible Tibetan plateau, and the lives of many inhabitants remain virtually untouched by the outside world.

PREVIOUS PAGE In 1993, driving south toward Lhasa, I gazed westward at Tuotuo He, an important tributary of the Yangtze River. River volume fluctuates throughout the year, frequently revealing sandbars. Fifty km (31 mi) upriver, Tuotuo He makes a 90-degree turn into a glacier valley, the true source of the mighty Yangtze. Beyond here lies Tuotuo Heyan, a truckstop town in southern Qinghai, and the 5,231 meter (17,162 ft) Tanggula Pass, one of two major hurdles to be crossed on the Qinghai–Tibet highway.

ABOVE This river at 4,500 meters (14,764 ft) parallels a road through the Aksai Chin, in western Tibet's Ali prefecture. In the late 1950s, the Chinese built the road, an important transport and supply route between Tibet and Xinjiang. Traversing disputed territory on the China–India border, the road has sparked numerous conflicts.

Run-off from the 12.5 km (7.75 mi) long Jianggendiru Glacier flows into the Tuotuo He and onward to the 6,380 km (3,964 mi) Yangtze. In 1985 I investigated eight other glaciers in this area. Tibetan nomads graze their livestock up to the tongue of the glacier, at an altitude of more than 5,000 meters (16,404 ft).

Their horses, these hardy little animals, that live on dry meat, tsam-pa, and tea leaves, stand beside their sleeping masters, their backs turned to the raging wind.
—*George N. Roerich, 1931*

LEFT In 1985, I encountered these horses en route to Tuotuo He, Qinghai. Gelandandong, the highest peak of the Tanggula Range, lies beyond. Even in summer, morning frost is an almost daily occurrence at 4,500 meters (17,164 ft) above sea level. Fifty Jiri Tibetans had gathered here for their annual horse-racing festivities.

ABOVE After eleven years without its foremost leader, the Karma Kagyu School of Tibetan Buddhism finally installed an eight-year-old boy as the 17th Karmapa, the highest reincarnated lama of the Kagyu-pa. The ceremony took place at Tsurphu Gonpa, 80 km (50 mi) northwest of Lhasa, on September 27, 1992. The second highest reincarnation of the Kagyupa, the Tai Situpa Rinpoche, traveled especially from India to officiate. At his installation before a crowd of 40,000, this young boy received a new name, Ugyen Trinley Dorje. While he sat in the lotus posture on his decorated throne, pilgrims made offerings to him of money, jewels, animal skins, butter, tea and a new truck. However, no one thought to bring the eight-year-old any toys.

The more inclement the weather, the better, for the merit acquired is therefore greater.
—Joseph Rock, 1956, on Tibetan pilgrims circumambulating
sacred mountain Anye Maqen

In 1921, British consular officer Eric Teichman called for further exploration of the little-known snow peaks of Qinghai, western Sichuan and Gansu, speculating that some mountains could "probably equal or surpass all but the highest giants of the Himalayas." In 1922, General George Pereira estimated the height of Qinghai's Anye Maqen Mountain at more than 7,575 meters (24,852 ft). Acting on that tip, botanist-adventurer Joseph Rock explored the slopes of Anye Maqen in 1925, estimating its height at 8,534 meters (28,000 ft).

In time, the legendary height of Anye Maqen swelled even more. American pilots flying supplies over the Hump during World War II reportedly looked up at the towering monstrosity while flying at a calculated altitude of 9,144 meters (30,000 ft)! This claim made Anye Maqen rank taller than Mount Everest, already a towering 8,848 meters (29,029 ft).

A Chinese team in the early 1970s finally confirmed the true height of Anye Maqen at 6,282 meters (20,610 ft), 30 percent lower than previous estimates. The area is sacred to Tibetan Buddhists, who make pilgrimages to circumambulate it by means of a path at the foot of the mountain. This act of religious devotion normally takes seven days, and is considered to benefit all sentient beings. Particularly devout pilgrims prostrate themselves the entire path, measuring out their body length along the ground with each step. The complete journey then takes two months. The Year of the Horse is the best time for this particular pilgrimage.

While most people think of Tibetans as purely nomadic, 80 percent of them live semi-sedentary lives and practice varying amounts of agriculture. This woman of the White Horse Valley prepares corn. The small group of 10,000 now known as "White-horse Tibetans," hopes that the government will recognize their existence as a separate nationality called the Di. While ancient Chinese historical records do mention Di people, all references to them end in AD 420. The Di inhabit a few villages in the Min Mountains between Nanping county in Sichuan and Wenxian in Gansu province—also home of the giant panda. Aside from the agricultural traditions of the Di, other distinguishing characteristics include their non-Tibetan baskets and unusual felt hats, which more closely resemble those of the Tu nationality in Huzhu, Qinghai. The Di people lack a written language but enjoy a colorful tradition of oral history.

Tsamba has much to recommend it, and if I were a poet I would write an ode to the stuff. It is sustaining, digestible, and cheap. For nearly three months we had tsamba *for breakfast and* tsamba *for lunch, and the diet was neither as unappetizing nor as monotonous as it sounds... I would not go so far as to say that you never get tired of* tsamba, *but you would get tired of anything else much quicker.*
—*Peter Fleming,* 1936

The high altitude of the Tibetan Plateau limits the variety of crops, making barley the staple food of the area. Highly versatile, this ancient grain grows at elevations of up to 4,600 meters (15,091 ft). Tibetans roast the barley kernels then grind them into flour. The *tsampa* is then mixed with butter-tea and rolled into a ball with the fingers to form a simple but filling meal. *Chang*, fermented barley beer, is the Tibetan national drink. Tibetans use soft barley straw as bedding, or as bulk roughage feed for their livestock during the winter months. In Zayu (Dzayul), southeastern Tibet near the Myanmar border, these Khampas harvest barley in preparation for the long winter.

ABOVE Already a capable young horseman, this boy rides home after a horseracing festival in southern Gansu's Maqu (Machu) County, home to 36,000 Tibetans. The sheepskin robe protects him from the high winds of the open steppe.

RIGHT In Zoige (Dzoge), Sichuan, a family of Tibetan nomads gathers sheep for shearing in August, 1988. The nomads stuff wool into sacks for later sale to traders, who come to buy the wool roadside.

Here are found many wild cattle that, in point of size, may be compared to elephants. Their colour is a mixture of white and black, and they are very beautiful to the sight. The hair upon every part of their bodies lies down smooth, excepting upon the shoulder, where it stands up to the height of about three palms. This hair, or rather wool, is white, and more soft and delicate than silk... Many of these cattle taken wild have been domesticated, and the breed produced between them and the common cow are nobler animals, and better qualified to resist fatigue than any other kind. They are accustomed to carry heavier burdens and to perform twice the labour in husbandry than could be derived from the ordinary sort, being both active and powerful.

—Marco Polo

LEFT A Tibetan man ploughs his fields with the aid of domestic yaks near Riwoqe (Riwoche), eastern Tibet. High rainfall makes the eastern plateau the breadbasket of Tibet.

RIGHT A Tibetan woman of the Golok ethnic group near Anye Maqen Mountain milks her family's yaks.

LEFT   A Tibetan woman shears sheep in Shannan, outside Cona, Tibet, southeast of Lhasa—an extremely poor area. The black felt hat with gold trim, embroidery and upturned corners is unique to that area.

Herders must be cautious in deciding when to shear their sheep, since weather on the Tibetan Plateau can be unpredictable. In July 1995,

nomads in the Khartan Valley of Aksai Kazak Autonomous County, Qinghai, gathered their sheep on the grasslands for shearing at the height of summer. That day, a hailstorm struck, chilling the naked sheep and killing a quarter of the herds. This unforeseen tragedy affected 39 of 40 Kazak families.

RIGHT   Even at an early age, nomad children learn to help their parents with chores. This Tibetan boy carries a calf away from its mother to be tied, so the cow can be milked.

After a short ride, the traveler notices several large black tents in a side valley, sheltered from the winds. Big, black dogs with large red and blue collars rush towards the road and bark fiercely. Tibet has a peculiar breed of enormous dogs, known to Europeans under the name of Tibetan mastiffs. They sometimes almost reach the size of a small donkey, with thick black fur, broad and powerful chest, and a huge head with powerful jaws. They are known to attack wolves, and I myself knew of one which successfully attacked a snow leopard. To render these animals less dangerous, the nomads tie up one of dog's front legs to its collar, making it impossible for him to attack and harm travelers. At night the dogs are let loose.
—George N. Roerich, 1931

Tibetans believe dogs to be reincarnations of those who strayed from Buddhism in a former life. Particularly ferocious mastiffs often chase our cars with great determination, attempting to sink their teeth into the rear bumpers. Fortunately, these two mastiffs near Anye Maqen offered no threat, plodding across the plain with several yaks and their herders.

Nomads gather at the Songke grasslands of southern Gansu for an annual festival. Tibetans have used these embroidered summer festival tents as protection from the elements for centuries. Their prized possessions accompany them, including a black and white television set, powered by a generator owned by a high-ranking lama in the next tent. I took this picture in 1982.

Domestic yak graze in the distance. China has 13 million, 93 percent of the world's total. Domesticated over 4,000 years ago, yaks provide the nomad with milk and meat for food, hair and wool for protection and *argul*, or dried dung, as fuel. Three to five lactating yaks, which give milk year round, easily provide enough milk, cheese and butter to sustain the average family.

On caravan, a yak covers about 15 km (9.3 mi) a day—sometimes over 5,000-meter (16,404-foot) passes—hauling up to 70 kilograms (154 lb). Yak caravan drivers control their animals by running, whistling and throwing stones using slings. *Lakto*, the Tibetan word for "yak driver," literally means, "hand with a stone."

The sure-footed yak is well suited to its harsh environment, withstanding temperatures as low as -40°C (-40°F). Standing two meters (6.5 ft) tall and weighing up to one ton (907 kg, or 2,000 lb), it has a lung capacity 1.4 percent of its total weight, versus 0.47 percent in lowland cattle, to handle the high altitude at which it works. Larger ribcages—15 pairs of ribs to a cow's 13 pairs—help accommodate large lungs. Underdeveloped sweat glands and a shaggy coat protect the beast against the cold. Moreover, three times more red blood cells than are found in lowland cows ensure that the yak gets enough oxygen from the rarefied air of the plateau. Problems arise only when yaks descend to altitudes lower than 3,000 meters (9,843 ft) and are subjected to diseases not common at higher elevations.

Fully 27 percent of all "beef" consumed in China is yak meat; 85,000 tons of yak meat was sold annually in China during the early 1980s. The fat content of yak's creamy yellowish milk runs from six to eight percent, versus 3.5 percent in cows. Yaks provide 20 percent of the milk consumed in China.

"You cannot compare us Go-log with other people... You are afraid of everyone... We Go-log, on the other hand, have from time immemorial obeyed none but our laws, none but our own convictions. A Go-log is born with the knowledge of his freedom, and with his mother's milk imbibes some acquaintance with his laws. They have never been altered. Almost in his mother's womb he learns to handle arms. His forebears were warriors—were brave fearless men, even as we today are their worthy descendants... Our tribe is the most respected and mighty in Tibet, and we rightly look down with contempt on both Chinaman and Tibetan."
—Speech made by Golok tribesman quoted by Joseph Rock, 1956

This Tibetan woman of the Washi-Golok ethnic group, between Litang and Yajiang (Nyachuka) in western Sichuan, adorns herself in their unique Golok style. A pair of inverted silver cups (*yinbingjiao*), which lie over her 108 braids, announce her married status. On her back, two prayer boxes (*gawo*) contain mantras or spiritual items blessed by a Rinpoche, incarnate lama, to protect against harm. Living in a difficult environment, Tibetans have always armed themselves both physically and spiritually with appropriate weapons, from knives, swords and rifles, to charm boxes, prayer wheels and rosaries.

In Tibetan, Golok has two meanings, literally "head on backwards" and "rebel." Numbering about 90,000, the Goloks are no strangers to war. Sent with neighboring Khampas to defend Tibet's northern frontier against a Chinese invasion in the seventh century, the Goloks later stayed in their mountain enclave in defiance of authorities. Their ways have changed little since then, their language unintelligible to most other Tibetans. The semi-nomadic Washi-Goloks view Anye Maqen as a sacred peak and live in close proximity to the mountain.

Yak carcasses line the road in Yushu (Jyekundo) Tibetan Autonomous Prefecture for government teams to assess damage and arrange for compensation, after catastrophic snowstorms ravaged Qinghai during the winter of 1995–96. Some families lost entire herds, sold what little they owned and moved as beggars to nearby towns. In the milder climate of Longbaotang, Pancho Quida lost 110 of 238 yaks, while Caiwen lost 37 of 59 yaks. Tax records throughout Tibetan history have chronicled the effects of these infrequent but devastating snowstorms.

Tibetans think that meteorological phenomena are the work of demons or magicians. A hail-storm is one of their favorite weapons. The former use it to hinder pilgrims on their journey to holy places and the latter, by this means, defend their hermitages from intruders and keep off faint-hearted candidates for discipleship.
—Alexandra David-Neel, 1932

Another severe blizzard struck northern Tibet on October 17, 1985. Dr. George Schaller noted its effect on local wildlife populations. Smaller animals such as gazelle and antelope had difficulty finding food in the deep snow; many died of starvation. Schaller found over 193 antelope bodies in one valley alone.

For two years after the blizzard, few antelope had the strength to breed. Larger animals, such as the wild ass, fared slightly better. Domestic livestock were affected as well, with families losing two-thirds of their sheep and goats and half their yak herds.

The traveler again journeys for several days without finding even a trace of human beings. Then one day, he may see a huge herd of black and brown domestic yaks coming down the mountain slope. Wild looking men in gray sheep-skin coats drive the herd. They circle about their animals, sometimes whistling, sometimes making peculiar shrill sounds that cut the rarefied atmosphere. These men wear no head covering and their long unkempt tresses play in the wind. All of the men are busy making strings out of sheep wool, which they roll between the palms of the hands and then twirl on small pieces of wood. This is the favorite occupation of nomads while driving their herds or squatting at camp fires. The presence of a herd of domestic yaks indicates that a nomad encampment is some-where near.

—*George N. Roerich, 1931*

Near the headwaters of the Yellow River in southeastern Qinghai, south of the Bayan Har Mountains, a yak caravan sets camp for the night during the first snow of winter. Tibetans use the conical tent only as a temporary shelter. These require only one pole to erect, as opposed to the more elaborate black felt tents, which can house a whole family all year round.

If a calf is born and dies, the mother's milk dries up at once unless the [nomads] do something to deceive her into thinking that her baby is still alive. It is the universal custom to stuff the dead calf's skin and prop it up against the cow each milking time. Then the milker milks with the calf held close against the cow while the mother licks and fondles it. Cows go off to graze every morning and leave their calves at the encampment, and they are accustomed to see them only at the milking time; consequently this ruse works surprisingly well. A cow will give milk until she has another calf if the stuffed body is presented to her each milk time.

—*Frans August Larson, 1930*

ABOVE A teenage Tibetan girl milks a yak on a frosty morning in Hongyuan, south of Zoige, in northwestern Sichuan. The calf is tied nearby the mother to stimulate milk production. Some Tibetans only milk three teats, leaving the fourth teat for calves alone.

OPPOSITE PAGE Tibetan families move camp on the back of their yaks— indispensable beasts of burden.

ABOVE At the conclusion of *Lung ta* festivities, this young boy begins the long ride home.

RIGHT Tibetan horsemen gather atop a sacred hillside in Maqu to sanctify the mountain gods and spread good fortune. One of seven counties of Gansu's Tibetan Autonomous Prefecture, Maqu is home to over 300,000 Tibetans. At the all-male event called *La Blasas*, horsemen release papers depicting the sacred Wind Horse (*Lung ta*). Meanwhile, burning juniper is offered as incense amidst a cacophony of battle cries, the firing of rifles and the frenzy of galloping horses—a throwback to Bon, Tibet's pre-Buddhist animistic religion. Symbolizing good fortune, each *Lung ta* paper portrays a fleet-footed horse carrying a flaming jewel to fulfill all wishes. Mythological animals in the corners signify the desire to spread good fortune to all beings, with holy mantras to invoke strength, wisdom and compassion. Tibetans release such *Lung ta* in high mountain passes to invoke the protection of mountain gods.

ABOVE In Songgang, Sichuan, just 12 km west of Barkham (Markam) and northwest of Chengki, Jiarong (Gyarong) Tibetans make their homes in fortress-like dwellings. Contrary to the image of the roving nomad, fully 80 percent of China's 4.6 million Tibetans lead a sedentary life. Although many Tibetan houses have mud walls, those in Barkham, Heishui and Daocheng are built of stone. Tibetan-style defense towers with six to eight sides preside over the town as reminders of past battles.

RIGHT A young boy scales a star-shaped defense tower in Barkham. These intricate towers, dating from the Qing dynasty (1644–1911), have no entrance on the ground floor and are accessed by ladder. Underground tunnels link some of the eight-storey towers; other secret tunnels lead to the river, ensuring a constant supply of fresh water. Often found in valley junctions, such towers exist only in the three neighboring counties of Barkham, Jinchuan (Chuchen) and Danba (Rongtrak) in Sichuan.

The Tibetan women were to us an especial object of interest, conspicuous in their long, bright colored dresses fastened around the waist by green or red sashes, their clumsy top-boots and their elaborate head dress. The hair was done up in a number of small plaits which hung down the back and were fastened together with wide strips of gay colored cloth, or by a heavy band of pasteboard or felt covered with silver ornaments, shells and beads, and on top of it all was a hat with white-fur brim and red tassels hanging from the pointed crown. From the ears were pendant great rings, to which were attached strings of beads hanging from long loops across the breast.

—Susie Rijnhart, 1901

Headdresses of the Jiarong Tibetan women of Heishui (Trochu) resemble those of the Liangshan Yi.

The Tibetans... are fond of decorating the bridges, the roads, and the peculiarly beautiful sites of their country with the inscriptions of a religious, philosophical, or poetic character. Some travellers have thought proper to ridicule that custom. I find it impossible to follow them. A few lines of delicate poetry, a page of a philosophical treatise such as one sees engraved on certain rocks in Thibet, the meditative image of a Buddha painted in a natural cave, or even a strip of paper hung above a river and swinging in the air at the top of a pass... seem to me greatly preferable to the advertisements of whiskey or ham which "decorate" the roads of Western countries.

—Alexandra David-Neel, 1927

Prayer flags in Serta, Sichuan, flutter in the breeze, wafting prayers up to heaven. Tibetan monks print cloths with text from Buddhist sutras and hang them, a meritorious act thought to help all sentient beings. Prayer wheels and huge *mani* piles—stacks of carved stones bearing the mystical mantra "Om Mani Padme Hum"—Hail the Jewel in the Lotus—serve the same purpose. Tibetan Buddhists hang prayer flags throughout Tibet, but only in the east do they hang them in this spiraling fashion.

Teachers and students gather before the monastic complex at Zhuqing (Dzogchen) Gonpa, a famous but well-hidden scholastic center in Juquen, northeast of Dege (Derge) in the Ganzi (Garze) Tibetan Autonomous Prefecture, western Sichuan. Zhuqing Monastery lies at the end of a winding dirt road at 3,900 meters (12,795 ft). Many of the monks shown here carry Tibetan Buddhist scriptures, printed with wooden blocks on long rectangular sheaves of paper, kept in carved wooden covers.

Animals are sensitive beings, differing in degree, not in kind, from ourselves, and must be treated accordingly—so runs [Tibetan] teaching. Hunting and fishing are discountenanced by the law, and foreigners admitted into Tibet are obliged to give a pledge that they will respect this prohibition. Wild animals are in consequence often very tame. Feeding of birds and fishes is considered a pious act. Meat-eating, though general because of the scarcity of other kinds of food in the plateau, is indulged as a regrettable necessity, but never defended, and the stricter lamas and any others who abstain from it altogether are much respected.

—*Marco Pallis, 1949*

Destroyed in the late 1950s, the monastery lay in ruins until 1983 when its leader, Garzhong Rinpoche, began reconstruction. The local government contributed 20,000 yuan for start-up costs.

First built in 1684–85 by a disciple of the Fifth Dalai Lama, Zhuqing Gonpa is considered one of the most important monasteries of the Nyingma sect in Kham, along with Baiyu Gonpa and Gartok Gonpa. Zhuqing has historically attracted many great scholars and maintains particular ties to monasteries in Bhutan.

The Lamaseries... are all constructed of brick and stone... The temples are general-
ly built with considerable elegance, and with great solidity; but these monuments
always seem crushed, being too low in proportion to their dimensions. Around the
Lamasery rise, numerous and without order, towers or pyramids, slender and
tapering, resting generally on huge bases, little in harmony with the tenuity of
the constructions they support. It would be difficult to say to what order of
architecture the Buddhic temples of Tartary belong. They are always fantastical
constructions of monstrous colonnades, peristyles with twisted columns, and end-
less ascents. Opposite the great gate is a kind of altar of wood or stone, usually in
the form of a cone reversed; on this the idols are placed, mostly seated cross-legged.
These idols are of colossal stature, but their faces are fine and regular, except in the
preposterous length of the ears...

—M. Huc, 1846

I crawled out of my sleeping bag in pre-dawn darkness to capture an early spring snow covering Palpung Gonpa. Many consider the *cholak-hang* (main assembly hall) one of the finest examples of classical Tibetan monastic architecture in western Sichuan; it is often called the "little Potala Palace." This building houses chanting rooms, classrooms and quarters for monastery leaders. In the foreground are ordinary monks' living quarters, called *chakhang.*

Traditional Tibetan buildings are made from local materials such as stone, wood and earth. Although the results are both attractive and functional, the limitations of these materials, combined with traditional design, make interiors dark and poorly ventilated.

In 1958, the government evicted many monks and closed most monasteries in this area. However, because Palpung's buildings proved useful as offices for government trade and administration, the structure was preserved. Religious activities at Palpung Gonpa resumed in 1982.

In 1991, I initiated a project with the China Exploration and Research Society (CERS) to preserve the architecture of Palpung monastery. Dr. Pamela Logan has managed the project since 1994. In September 1997, the World Monuments Fund announced the selection of Palpung Monastery for the World Monuments Watch 1998–99, a list of 100 of the World's Most Endangered Sites.

Recognized as one of the most important centers of the Karma Kagyu Sect of Tibetan Buddhism, Palpung welcomes many pilgrims and students from afar. A road completed in 1997 ended centuries of isolation for the monastery. Previously one could reach Palpung Monastery only after a half-day's horseback ride over two 4,000-meter mountain passes. Three hours south of Palpung lies Baiya Gonpa in the Ganzi Tibetan Autonomous Prefecture, another monastery CERS is preserving in cooperation with the local population.

Like the neighboring Mongols, Tibetans in the highlands of Gansu practice a traditional "mountain-god offering" ceremony, an early summer ritual reminiscent of Tibet's animist origins. At a sacred mountain, eight miles from the Buddhist monastery of Labrang, one long, colorful stave, like an arrow, is planted within a circle for each family. Nomads make offerings of yak butter and *tsampa*, the Tibetan staple of parched barley. Historically, only men attended such ceremonies, as women were thought to bring bad luck. Much merriment accompanies the celebration, including the blowing of conch shell horns and the staccato of wild gunfire.

The melody [of the monastic orchestra] flowed as smoothly as the water of a deep river, without interruption, emphasis or passion. It produced a strange, acute impression of distress, as if all the suffering of the beings wandering from world to world, since the beginning of the ages, was breathed out in this weary, desperate lamentation. What musician, inspired without his knowing, had found this leit motiv *of universal sorrow? And how, with this heterogeneous orchestra, could men devoid of any artistic sense render it with such heart-rending fervour?—This remained a mystery...*

—*Alexandra David-Neel, 1932*

LEFT   A monk plays a ceremonial trumpet at Yushu (Jyekundo) as part of a Buddhist orchestra, accompanying dancers engaged in a three-day festival of religious dance dramas (*cham*) for the local nomads. The instruments of Tibetan ritual music are completely different from those for secular use. Although limited to drums, cymbals and trumpets, these temple orchestras assume a power all their own, creating unearthly sounds transcending the rhythm of this world. As with other Tibetan ritual objects, the use of ornate precious metal and wood takes on special significance.

RIGHT   Two young monks of the temple orchestra in Serta blow horns made of conch shells—to announce the commencement of festivities. The ritual bronze bell, or *dril-bu*, is used in conjunction with a *dorje*, or "diamond scepter," representing the thunderbolt, a symbol of power. Held in the left and right hands, respectively, the ceremonial instruments represent the mystical union of wisdom and compassion. A pair of trumpets inlaid with coral and turquoise, rest beyond. The bespectacled monk holds a green *damaru*, a double-headed leather drum sometimes made from human skulls and covered in snakeskin. Behind rest telescopic trumpets, which always appear in pairs.

157

Tibetan monks from various local monasteries gather at Serta (Sertal), western Sichuan, to celebrate the consecration of a 50 meter-high *chorten*, said to represent the five elements into which the body is resolved at death: earth, air, fire, water and ether. One of the few areas to remain separate from Chinese imperial government or Lhasa rule, Serta functioned under the tribal system of Golok nomads until the 1950s. This gathering of Gelukpa sect monks listens to low, haunting sounds of ceremonial telescopic horns. Musicians manipulate the sound in such trumpets solely by vibration of lips and breath control.

Only high officials of the Gelukpa sect wear the yellow crested hats shown here. Imported to Tibet in the seventh century, Tibetan Buddhists have borrowed liberally from the indigenous animist faith of Bon.

South of Lanzhou, the capital of Gansu, monks engage in philosophical discussion at Labrang Monastery, a Gelukpa sect monastery prominent as a major theological center since 1709. Labrang is home to six colleges and once maintained a student body of 3,000 monks. Its authority extends to 47 other Gelukpa monasteries in the region. During the first half of this century one in four Tibetan men lived in celibacy in such lamaseries, helping reduce the population of Tibet to 1.3 million by 1957. Since the 1960s, a decline in the number of lamas has resulted in steady population growth.

LEFT During a summer festival in Yushu, the "white old man," called Tsagan Obogen, performs crowd control in a comical way, pushing revellers back with his highly stylized movements. He uses the pillow of imitation leopard skin, draped across his shoulders, as a baton to beat members of the crowd. Bystanders enjoy the antics of this comical character mingling with the crowd and mimicking the actors.

MIDDLE At a festival at Renzhen Monastery in Serxu, northeast of Lhasa, a demon figure represents a guardian king from pre-Buddhist times.

RIGHT Sven Hedin remarked that masked religious dances, a throw-back to ancient Bon practices, probably once included human sacrifices. Today, one such dance involves the dismemberment of a human-shaped clay figure, which the Deer Mask dancer symbolically cuts into small pieces.

OPPOSITE PAGE This audience at the Serxu festival has a bird's eye view of the monks' dramatic performances.

LEFT The highly stylized *Shanag Cham* (Black Hat Dance) is usually performed for the Great Prayer Festival (*Monlam Chenmo*) in the first month of the lunar year. Perched atop the felt hat wrapped in velvet are two snakes guarding a precious jewel. The dance commemorates the assassination in AD 890 of iconoclast King Langdarma by Lama Pal-dorje.

RIGHT In the *Durdak Garcham* (Cemetery Lords Dance), monks remind their audience of the ephemeral nature of all things. A fast and joyous dance, it symbolizes release from the delusion of things static and concrete.

Each year, Tibetans hold a summer festival on the seventh day of the seventh month at Norbulingka, the summer palace of the Dalai Lama, in Lhasa. Because this is the residence of Tibet's spiritual leader, no drinking, gambling or smoking is permitted. Here Tibetan nomads play mahjong in an elaborately decorated white tent, with a double canopy for extra shade against the hot summer sun.

At 4,000 meters (13,123 ft) above sea level, Litang is one of the highest county towns east of Tibet proper, and one of two sites in western Sichuan to host massive nomadic festivities every August. In this horseback game, Tibetan men—here the great Khampa warriors of eastern Tibet—race to pick up *khatas*, white scarves used in religious ceremonies, from the ground. In such remote areas where mobility is of utmost importance, Tibetans value good horses. A Tibetan saying goes, "A horse which cannot carry a man uphill is not a good horse; a man who rides a horse downhill is not a good man." Although this festival is not associated with any monastery, Litang is a famous site of Tibetan Buddhism. Both the Seventh and Tenth Dalai Lamas were born here, and the first Gelukpa monastery of Kham was built here 400 years ago.

[The Tibetans] look fine seated on their mules with their daggers, their broadswords inset with precious stones, and our magazine rifles slung over their shoulders. On their heads they wear fur caps, and their necks, ears and fingers are adorned with silver rings. Their large reliquaries jolt against the left side of their bodies, and their right sleeves, which in Tibetan fashion they wear loose, hang elegantly down against the rights flanks of their horses.

—André Guibaut, 1948

Tibetan nomads wear their best for the Langshan Festival, an annual summer gathering. The festivities just north of Serxu (Sershul), northwestern Sichuan, include tug-of-war, wrestling, yak and horse races, and a parade of jeeps and motorcycles. Tibetans use such gatherings as an opportunity to display their wealth, from machine-guns and knives to the finest of horses and jewels. Due to dwindling wildlife populations, imitation fur has replaced the traditional leopard or otter skin on the trim of the horseman's robe.

Two horsemen at a festival in Serxu. The brilliant horse-blanket and rug are in typical Tibetan style, with multi-colored lines along the edge.

Snuff, a fine mixture of tobacco and ash, decorates this man's nose. Although using snuff is not unlike sniffing red hot pepper—the very

thought brings tears to my eyes— I have found it to be the best decongestant available on the plateau.

The Tibetan's gun is his most valued possession. It is a matchlock with a long fork which pivots around a screw through the stock. The barrel and all the iron work are made by the Chinese, but the Tibetans often make the stock, using very light wood which they sometimes cover with wild-ass skin... They can make very good shooting with them at the average range of about 100 yards, but I never saw them hit a moving object, although some of them said they could. These Koko-nor Tibetans do not attach as much value to swords as do the people of eastern Tibet (K'amdo), and usually carry only common ones of Chinese make, with wooden scabbards.

—William Woodville Rockhill, 1891

Aside from modern semi-automatics, many Tibetans own old matchlock rifles with stabilizing prongs. Matchlock guns prevailed in Tibet from the 16th century until the introduction of British rifles in 1904.

At 7,556 meters (24,790 ft), Minya Gongga (Minyak Gangkar) in western Sichuan is the seventh highest mountain in the world. This king of Sichuan's mountains—a sacred peak to Tibetans—is the highest peak east of the Himalayas. Botanist Joseph Rock explored Mount Gongga with a team of local helpers in 1929 but insisted on circling the foot of the mountain in the opposite direction to religious pilgrims.

When an unseasonal hailstorm ruined the barley crop later that season, local farmers were quick to blame Rock for upsetting the mountain gods.

The isolation of Mount Gongga

has protected its wildlife from the destruction wrought elsewhere in China, with deer, blue sheep, takin and black bears still prevalent, as well as a variety of bird life.

However, the demand for wild animal parts for use in traditional Chinese and Tibetan medicine makes some species' continued survival precarious.

TOP   Part of the Konkaling range in western Sichuan, sacred mountains Chanodorji, pictured here, and Jambeyang each rise 5,958 meters (19,547 ft) above sea level.

LEFT The northeast face of Shenrezi, viewed from Konka Chonggu monastery in western Sichuan, stands 6,032 meters (19,790 ft) above sea level. Tibetan Buddhists believe the Dalai Lama to be the incarnation of Shenrezi, the all-compassionate one. Along with Chanodorji and Jambeyang, the three sacred snow peaks represent deities of the Buddhist pantheon. Named by the Fifth Dalai Lama, these holy mountains attract countless pilgrims, who circumambulate the base of the mountains.

RIGHT At 11 years old, Thupten Jurong has already recited more Buddhist sutras than his four elder teachers combined. With a calm mien and intelligence that belies his age, the young *trapa* will take charge of Konka Chonggu Monastery when he grows up. While other young boys might dream of the city, Thupten Jurong is content to study scriptures in this pristine area called Konkaling.

OPPOSITE PAGE An alpine stream winds through pasture below the sacred peak of Chanodorji. My team shared the campsite with tribal warriors sent to assert rights to a gold mine. Luckily we avoided any crossfire.

ABOVE The symmetrical pyramid Xinjingnaray rises over the sacred lake Jomonachu, next to snow peak Shenrezi. This view at 3,905 meters (12,812 ft) greeted me after a short hike through lush, virgin forest behind Konka Chonggu Monastery.

LEFT One of my assistants, Liu Hong, displays a photograph of Joseph Rock's Konkaling campsite, from his 1931 *National Geographic* article, "Holy Mountains of the Outlaws." The glacial moraine has changed little in almost 70 years.

ABOVE I encountered this devout pilgrim woman circumambulating the sacred peaks of Konkaling, near Jambeyang. Joseph Rock often noted that Tibetans strongly resembled North America's Apache Indians.

RIGHT In 1997, I hired 13 horses, one Tibetan interpreter and three caravan helpers to lead my team from Kanggu village up the Konka River gorge, destined for the sacred mountains of Konkaling.

Daocheng (Dapba) Tibetan warriors pose with their rifles under the shadow of Chanodorji. A tribal dispute over gold mining rights has neighboring counties of Daocheng and Muli up in arms. In this remote corner of Sichuan, a traditionally Tibetan area, local governments have sent these warriors to battle, taking matters into their own hands. Advising on the danger of being caught in crossfire, Wangden Tseren, deputy commander of the Riwa township militia, warned us, "Bullets have no eyes."

The Grand Lama appears to be about sixty. Like all the priests of his creed, he wears his hair short, and being beardless by nature, he has no need to shave. His features are regular, especially by comparison with those of his doctor. He has rather a broad face, but the black eyes are very intelligent, the mouth is delicate, and the eyelids very clearly defined. He is easy in his gestures, and has a good deal of unction in his voice.

—Gabriel Bonvalot, 1891

Reja, a 62-year-old *khan-po*, or head lama, single-mindedly rebuilt Konka Chonggu Monastery eight years ago. With three other adult monks and one young and intelligent *trapa*, or student monk, Reja maintains the paradise he rebuilt in a pristine environment and looks after the pilgrims who trek to this remote site.

HIMALAYAN FOOTHILLS

On the southern rim of the Tibetan Plateau, the Himalayas extend 2,414 km (1,497 mi) across Asia through Kashmir, northern India, Tibet, Nepal, Sikkim and Bhutan. The range boasts nine of the world's ten highest peaks and is among the youngest geological formations in the world; crust upheavals started only some 30 million years ago. Seismic activity frequently rocks the region; scars on the hillside near Zayu serve as reminders of an 8.6-scale earthquake on August 15, 1950. The northern foothills of the Himalayas occupy a band of China's Yunnan province, an area remarkably diverse both in landscape and culture.

With its source on the flanks of Tibet's sacred Mount Kailash, the Yarlung Tsangpo River flows east, tracing a course along the northern foothills. At Mount Namjagbarwa, whose peak is the region's highest at 7,756 meters (25,446 ft), the river makes a dramatic hairpin turn to the west. Here it carves out one of the deepest gorges in the world, with a vertical drop of some 5,000 meters (16,500 ft). This canyon divides the Himalayas from the Hengduan Mountains to the east. Finally the river drops down to the plains of India, where it is known as the Brahmaputra, before emptying into the Bay of Bengal.

A variety of ethnic people dwell in the Himalayan foothills, where they are isolated by towering mountains and deep river gorges. These groups include the Deng, Lhoba and Lisu, as well as the Naxi and matriarchal Moso people, all of whom maintain distinct traditional cultures.

Bomi (Po-me) in southeast Tibet is located on the southern route connecting western Sichuan with Lhasa. The route is little used owing to the steep terrain and frequent landslides during summer monsoons.

PREVIOUS PAGE Snow mountain near Zayu, southeastern Tibet.

ABOVE With an elevation less than 3,000 meters (9,843 ft), Bomi hosts the world's northernmost tropical rain forest, at a latitude of 29 degrees. Other rain forests in China lie below 20 degrees on Hainan Island, and near 22 degrees in Mengla, Yunnan.

OPPOSITE PAGE Bomi Tibetans live within a loop of the Yarlung Zangbo in Bomi, southeastern Tibet, near the border with India. Here the river makes a hairpin turn at Mount Namjagbarwa cutting a deep gorge before dropping into the plains of India to the south. Bomi people are more akin to Lhoba and other ethnic groups of the Indian sub-continent than to other Tibetans. Independent until the 1920s, the Bomi wear a simple vest like their Lhoba neighbors, unlike the tradi-tional Tibetan robe.

The Deng people of Zayu (Dzayul) are so remote that they did not receive the county telephone service until 1989. Roughly 1,000 individuals comprise the Deng people, who are not yet recognized as a nationality in China. Common law among the Deng resolves disputes, taking precedence over state mandates. Deng women wear a silver hair band engraved with flowers and cylinder-shaped earrings with whorl patterns, and often smoke a silver pipe. Remote Zayu, one of Tibet's subtropical areas, lies near the sensitive Myanmar and Indian border.

OPPOSITE PAGE The 2,300 Lhoba within China inhabit a few villages near Mainling (Menling), southeastern Tibet, within a loop of the Brahmaputra River. One of the few non-Buddhist nationalities in Tibet, the Lhoba are animists. Aside from growing wheat and barley, they also hunt, accompanied by dogs. The meat obtained is distributed equally among the community. To determine hunting fortunes, Lhoba elders use bamboo sticks to slice open young chickens and then "read" the grains of the giblets at a miniature bamboo altar. Lhoba have very little in the way of songs or music, although I did document one ritualistic hunting dance. The singer holds a knife in his hand, as if chopping in time to the sentences, which he speaks more than sings.

LEFT This young Lhoba hunter has abandoned his traditional clothing (see right) in favor of a more modern style.

RIGHT The bow and arrow of the Lhoba hold special significance. Unlike the more common crossbow, this bamboo bow is held upright. The arrowhead is selected according to the animal to be hunted. This skilled Lhoba hunter holds a second arrow ready with his little finger. Older hunters wear hats of woven rattan with bearskin trim; younger men have adopted woolen fedoras. The shells around this hunter's waist were once used as currency.

ABOVE　Lhoba poison arrows are treated with a natural plant-derived poison strong enough to kill a full-grown Burmese tiger. The poison used is probably similar to the *Aconitum* species used by the Lisu nationality. Tested in the laboratory, this poison—*caowu* in Chinese— acts like *curare*, used by Amazon Indians, and has been developed into a modern anesthetic.

OPPOSITE PAGE　At an elevation of more than 2,600 meters (8,530 ft), this winding road along the Mekong River in Deqen, in the northwestern corner of Yunnan, keeps local road crews busy year-round. Built on soft rocks, which provide a poor foundation, the road is susceptible to landslides triggered by monsoon rains. The resultant roadblocks halt traffic for days at a time, as I have learned during frequent summer trips across the Tibetan Plateau.

Steel cables enable the stout of heart to cross the Mekong River. Gravity carries the passenger only halfway across the single cable "bridge," at which point the individual must draw himself hand over hand to the opposite shore. Despite this primitive means of river crossing, the riverbank opposite boasts a small hydroelectric plant and several small villages.

These Lisu villagers of Fugong County, Yunnan, live apart from their kinsmen in an isolated settlement along the Salween River near the Myanmar border. The rest of China's 574,600 Lisu are found in northwest Yunnan, a mountainous area with dense fir forests. Lisu traditionally followed animistic practices, but adopted Christianity and Catholicism in the mid-19th century. Traditional bow hunting, involving the use of poison arrows, helps to supplement a diet of maize and buckwheat, with oxen and pigs slaughtered for major festivals.

Burdened with the loads of mushrooms and bunches of flowers we sat down to rest or lay upon the Tibetan rugs we had brought. It was wonderfully peaceful in these lonely mountains. There were no sounds but the whispering of pines and singing of birds. I was assured there were many nagas and fairies living in this endless forest. Afterwards we descended to a little spring of water gurgling out of a huge rock.
—Peter Goullart, 1955

Mount Kawa Karpo, a sacred, glacier-capped peak of 6,702 meters (21,988 ft), lies between the Salween and Mekong Rivers. The mountain's western flank stands in Tibet, the foothills in Yunnan's pine forests to the east. Its glacier descends to 2,200 meters (7,218 ft), the lowest of any glacier in the northern hemisphere in both altitude and latitude. Tibetans consider the mountain sacred and climbing is forbidden here. The Year of the Sheep is thought to be most auspicious for circumambulating the base.

Just ten km (6.2 mi) north of Yanjing at Qujika, along the Mekong River, steam rises from a natural hot spring. Local Tibetans wash their laundry here year-round and consider the water beneficial for skin diseases, intestinal disorders and rheumatism, to name a few. Note the ancient swastika symbol on the roof of a bathhouse. Drawn by Buddhists in a clockwise direction, a swastika is one of the 32 symbols of excellence to be found on a Buddha's body. The inverse swastika is a symbol of Bon, the animistic tradition prevalent in Tibet before the coming of Buddhism in the seventh century.

This hidden valley was surely one of the most beautiful places in the world. At least 8,000 feet up, it was hemmed in by great snow mountains and the climate was a perpetual spring. Two roaring torrents of pure glacier water cascaded down both sides of the valley. There were vast forests on the foothills: carpets of flower covered alpine meadows and clearings in the forest: some of the rarest lilies in the world grew wild among the ridges: the air was heavy with the fragrance of so many flowers, myriads of bees buzzed around and the soil was black and rich. The Catholic mission had all kinds of fruit-bearing trees in its orchards and vegetables of all descriptions in the well laid-out and watered gardens.

—Peter Goullart, 1955

ABOVE   Xi Deyong, a 78-year-old visiting priest, looks after the 140-year-old Catholic church in Yanjing, Tibet. Founded by French missionaries in the 1860s, Lagong Church uses Tibetan language bibles and hymnbooks printed in 1894. Today 87 local families practice Christianity. Note the multi-storied Tibetan houses in background.

OPPOSITE PAGE   Another Catholic church just down the river from Lagong Church in Yanjing.

But [they] stopped for another day in the great salt city of Yen Gin, where salt has been procured for two thousand years. This salt is carried up out of shallow, narrow salt-water wells by bare-footed women, up notched logs and poured on the flat top of the houses to dry. There is no machinery whatever, only the sun and wind to aid them.

—*Flora Beal Shelton, 1912*

Along the Mekong River in Yanjing, southeastern Tibet, local inhabitants harvest salt from deep wells, as they have for centuries. Carried out of the wells in heavy wooden buckets, the brine water is spread on shallow terraces to dry. The salt is then bundled in yak-hide bags for caravan transport across the plateau. An efficient transportation system moves the salt westward and eastward, respectively, with no crossover of territory.

The eponymous town on the lush western shore is called Hong Yanjing (Red Salt Well) for the pinkish salt it produces; the arid east bank Bai Yanjing (White Salt Well) for its white brine. At Hong Yanjing, the best salt is produced in March and called "Peach Blossom Salt" in reference to the coloration

and the season when peach flowers are in bloom.

Salt has long been important in the history of Inner Asia, not only for seasoning food but also as currency. Marco Polo described the use of salt as currency in the late 13th century. Dried cakes of salt bore the imprint of the seal of Kublai Khan, at great profit to the salt merchants. The further the salt traveled from its source, the more valuable it became—not unlike the chocolate bars or Kodak film I carry on expedition today. I often tell my team that the price of one roll of film increases one yuan per day. This can certainly add up on longer expeditions! Even today, by the time the salt travels 600 km (372 mi) from Yanjing to Dali, in Yunnan, its price increases fivefold.

OPPOSITE PAGE Fir trees protected by the Lijiang government grow up to the snow line on Jade Dragon (Yulong) Snow Mountain. While the Chinese usually view such evergreen forest as a resource to be harvested, local authorities now seek to preserve the area for tourism. This mountainous terrain is a classic example of previously glacier-covered rock.

ABOVE A Naxi tailor sews animal hides in his Lijiang workshop.

Between spells of business they sat on the doorsteps… embroidering, in multi-coloured silks, the seven stars which every Nakhi woman, married or unmarried, wears on the back of her traditional sheepskin jacket… The fur is inside and a woollen tippet of dark blue colour covers the shoulders on the outside. These pretty circlets are about two inches in diameter. Formerly there were two larger circlets, representing the sun and moon, but they were now no longer worn.
—*Peter Goullart, 1955*

Note the traditional, woman's Naxi cape hanging at right. Worn on the back over an outfit of blue or black, the cape prevents chafing when carrying baskets. The light and dark portions of the cape represent day and night.

The mighty Yangtze cascades through a series of rapids over 100 meters (328 ft) below the footpath at Tiger Leaping Gorge. These drop a dramatic 210 meters (689 ft) through a series of seven falls in the 17 km (11 mi) canyon. Depending on the season, the river ranges in width from 30 to 60 meters (98–197 ft)—a narrow span which once gave rise to the belief that a tiger could easily leap across —hence the gorge's name. Flanked by the 5,596-meter (18,360 ft) Yulong Snow Mountain to the east and the 4,700-meter (15,420 ft) Harba Snow Mountain to the west, the canyon plunges more than 3,000 meters (9,843 ft), creating one of the deepest gorges in the world.

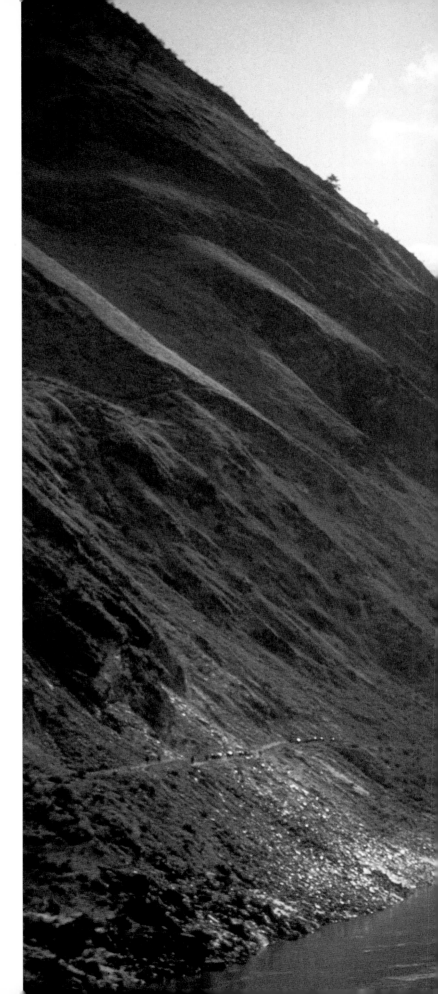

The Yungning country was a land of free love and all efforts of the Liukhi [Moso] women were concentrated on enticing more lovers in addition to their husbands. Whenever a Tibetan caravan or other strangers were passing Yungning, these ladies went into a huddle and secretly decided where each man should stay. The lady then commanded her husbands to disappear... She and her daughters prepared a feast and danced for the guest. Afterwards the older lady bade him to make a choice between riper experience and foolish youth.

—Peter Goullart, 1955

Friends of the United Nations chose Lige Village at Lugu Lake, northwestern Yunnan, as one of 50 global, model communities for the United Nations' 50th anniversary celebration in 1995. The Moso people of Lige are known for the high esteem placed on women and for the care of children.

The Moso live near Luguhu, along the Yunnan–Sichuan border. A matrilineal society, the Moso family name and inheritance pass through the mother's side. *Azhus*, or casual lovers, visit the women's households at night but return to their own homes during the day. Although the Moso are slowly adopting a patrilineal system, a 1983 survey showed that 393 of 1,878 mature Moso women still maintained *azhu* relationships. Children are raised by their mother and her brothers, and may not know their father at all.

Moso custom dictates an elaborate funeral ceremony for deceased matriarchs, which involves the cremation of the body on a funerary pyre not far from Lugu Lake. Qier, a Moso matriarch, passed away in January 1997 at the age of 79. We have studied her family several times since 1985, and hers was one of five households CERS selected for assistance in cultural conservation. Pictured on right, 25 shamans, called *dongba*, from nearby counties presided over the three-day ritual, which was held on a scale that had not been seen in 40 years. With modernization reaching even remote areas like Luguhu, I fear that such ancient traditions may not continue long into the future.

Situated near Yongning, on the
border of Yunnan and Sichuan,
Luguhu (Lugu Lake) is famous for
its pristine beauty and elevation in
the mountains. CERS is working
to document the ancient traditions
of the Moso, and recently helped
preserve these typical Moso village
houses. Eventually we hope to
help the Moso convert this into
a museum showcasing their
unique heritage.

The Moso regard Lioness Rock as
a goddess. Appropriately for this
matriarchal society, this hill representing a female deity towers over
other, smaller peaks in the area.
The Moso are a sub-group of the
Naxi striving for recognition as a
separate nationality.

ABOVE LEFT Yi men traditionally wear their hair in a protruding braid like this. The black felt cape, or *tsarwa*, which gathers at the neck, is distinctly Yi. Worn by men and women alike, the *tsarwa* provides protection from the elements, and doubles as a jacket and blanket.

ABOVE RIGHT Numbering 6.6 million, members of the Yi nationality, predominately from the Liangshan (Cool Mountains) Yi Autonomous Prefecture in southern Sichuan, relinquished their hierarchical slave society in the 1950s. A caste system previously divided them into Black Yi (nobles), White Yi (commoners), and two groups of slaves, the Ajia and Yaxi. While slavery has fallen by the wayside, ethnic costumes of the Yi have persisted to this day. Within the Yi nationality, some two million people are still called by their former, traditional name, the Lolo.

The Noble Lolos [Yi]…are very tall and of a regal bearing…Their eyes are large and liquid, with a fire burning in them…Their hair is black, slightly wavy and very soft; its arrangement is a distinctive feature of all Lolos. It is gathered through a hole at the top of their dark blue or black turbans and hangs like a limp tail, or, more often, springs up like a miniature palm tree, supported by a sheath of black strings. The hair of the Lolo is sacred, and no one is supposed to touch it under the pain of death. They believe that Divine Spirit communicates with man through the exposed lock of his hair which…conveys the spiritual impulses, like waves to a receiver, to the brain.

—Peter Goullart, 1955

ABOVE A Yi mother carries her child on her back. The embroidery on the woman's blouse and the silvery jangles on her infant's hat are indicative of her village.

LEFT　Snowflakes drift about village houses between Dali and Lijiang, in northwestern Yunnan. The area is home to many of China's ethnic peoples, including the Bai, Naxi and Yi people.

PREVIOUS PAGES　Yunnan's Jingpo people dress in full regalia to celebrate the Mulouzhong festival, parading and dancing to the rhythm of traditional instruments.

BIBLIOGRAPHY

Andrews, Roy Chapman. *On the Trail of Ancient Man*. New York: G.P. Putnam's Sons, 1926

Bailey, F.M. *China—Tibet—Assam*. London: Jonathan Cape, 1945

——. *No Passport to Tibet*. London: Travel Book Club, 1957

Bonvalot, Gabriel. *Across Thibet*. Translated by C.B. Pitman. 2 vols. London: Cassel, 1891. Reprinted, New York: Cassel, 1982

Bower, Hamilton. *Diary of a Journey Across Tibet*. New York: Macmillan, 1894. Reprinted, Kathmandu: Ratna Pustak Bhandar, 1976

Burdsall, R., A. Emmons, T. Moore, and J. Young. *Men Against the Clouds*. New York: Harper, 1935

Cable, Mildred, and Francesca French. *The Gobi Desert*. New York: Macmillan, 1944

——. *Through Jade Gate and Central Asia: An Account of Journeys in Kansu, Turkestan and the Gobi Desert*. Boston: Houghton Mifflin, 1927

Cobbold, Ralph P. *Innermost Asia: Travel and Sport in the Pamirs*. New York: Charles Scribner's Sons, 1900

Coleman, Graham, ed. *A Handbook of Tibetan Culture*. Boston: Shambhala, 1994

Das, Sarat Chandra. *Journey to Lhasa and Central Tibet*. London: John Murray, 1902. Reprinted, New Delhi: Asia Education Services, 1989

David-Neel, Alexandra. *Magic and Mystery in Tibet*. New York: Claude Kendall, 1932

——. *My Journey to Lhasa*. New York and London: Harper and Brothers, 1927. Reprinted, Boston: Beacon Press, 1993

Deasy, H. *In Tibet and Chinese Turkestan*. New York: Longmans Green, 1901

D'Ollone, Vicomte. *In Forbidden China: The D'Ollone Mission, 1906–1909, China–Tibet–Mongolia*. Translated by Bernard Miall. Boston: Small, Maynard and Co., n.d.

Easton, Robert. *China Caravans*. Santa Barbara: Capra Press, 1982

Farrer, Reginald. *On the Eaves of the World*. London: Edward Arnold and Co., 1917

Fleming, Peter. *Bayonets to Lhasa*. New York: Harper, 1961

——. *News from Tartary*. Los Angeles: J.P. Tarcher, 1936. Reprinted, London: Futura Publications, 1980

Fraser, David. *The Marches of Hindustan*. Edinburgh and London: W. Blackwood and Sons, 1907

Goldstein, Melvyn, and Cynthia Beall. *Nomads of Western Tibet*. Berkeley and Los Angeles: University of California Press, 1990

——. *The Changing World of Mongolia's Nomads*. Hong Kong: Odyssey, 1994

Goullart, Peter. *Land of the Lamas: Adventures in Secret Tibet*. New York: E.P. Dutton, 1959

——. *The Forgotten Kingdom*. London: John Murray, 1955

Grenard, Fernard. *Tibet: The Country and Its Inhabitants*. Translated by A.T. de Mattos. London: Hutchison, 1904

Grunfeld, A. Tom. *The Making of Modern Tibet*. Armonk, New York: M.E. Sharpe, 1996

Guibaut, André. *Tibetan Venture: In the Country of the Ngolo-Setas*. Translated by Lord Sudley. London: John Murray, 1948

Gyurme Dorje, ed. *Tibet Handbook with Bhutan*. Lincolnwood, Illinois: Passport Books, 1996

Hedin, Sven. *Across the Gobi Desert*. London: Routledge and Sons, 1931

——. *Central Asia and Tibet*. 2 vols. London: Hurst and Blackett, 1903

——. *My Life as an Explorer*. New York: Garden City Publishing, 1925

——. *The Chinese Lama Temple*. Chicago: Century of Progress Exposition, 1932

——. *The Silk Road*. London: Butler and Tanner, 1938

——. *Trans-Himalaya: Discoveries and Adventures in Tibet*. New York: Macmillan, 1909

Hopkirk, Peter. *Foreign Devils on the Silk Road*. London: Murray, 1980

——. *Trespassers on the Roof of the World*. Oxford: Oxford University Press, 1982

Huc, Evariste-Régis, and Joseph Gabet. *Travels in Tartary Thibet and China 1844-1846*. Translated by William Hazlitt. 2 vols. New York and London: Harper and Brothers, 1928

Kinnosuke, Adachi. *Manchuria: A Survey*. New York: Robert M. McBride and Company, 1925

Knox, Thomas W. *Overland Through Asia*. Hartford, Connecticut: American Publishing, 1873

Larson, Frans August. *Larson, Duke of Mongolia*. Boston: Little, Brown and Co., 1930

Lattimore, Owen. *Inner Asian Frontiers of China*. Broadway, New York: American Geographical Society, 1940

———. *Mongol Journeys*. New York: Doubleday, Doran and Co., 1941

———. *Studies in Frontier History*. London: Oxford University Press: 1962

Lias, Godfrey. *Kazak Exodus*. London: Evans Brothers, 1956

Maillart, Ella. *Turkestan Solo*. Translated by John Rodker. New York: G.P. Putnam's Sons, 1935

Mannin, Ethel. *South to Samarkand*. London: Jerrolds Publishers, 1936

Maxwell, Neville. *India's China War*. New York: Pantheon Books, 1970

Ossendowski, Ferdinand. *Beasts, Men and Gods*. New York: E.P. Dutton, 1922

Pallis, Marco. *Peaks and Lamas*. New York: Alfred A. Knopf, 1949

Polo, Marco. *The Travels of Marco Polo*. Revised from Marsden's translation. New York and London: Liveright, 1982

Prejevalsky, Colonel Nikolai. *From Kulja, Across the Tian Shan to Lob-Nor*. Translated by E. Delmar Morgan. London: Sampson, Low, Marston, Searle and Rivington, 1879

Qiu Pu. *The Oroqens: China's Nomadic Hunters*. Beijing: Foreign Languages Press, 1983

Rawling, C. *The Great Plateau*. London: Edward Arnold, 1905

Rijnhart, Susie C. *With the Tibetans in Tent and Temple*. Chicago: Fleming H. Revell, 1901

Rock, Joseph. *The Amnye Ma-Chhen Range and Adjacent Regions*. Rome: Is. M.E.O., 1956

Rockhill, William Woodville. *The Land of the Lamas*. New York: Century, 1891

Roerich, George N. *Trails to Inmost Asia*. New Haven: Yale University Press, 1931

Roerich, Nicholas. *Altai-Himalaya*. New York: Frederick A. Stokes, 1929

Roosevelt, Theodore, and Kermit Roosevelt. *East of the Sun—West of the Moon*. New York: Scribner's, 1926

Rowell, Galen. *Mountains of the Middle Kingdom*. San Francisco: Sierra Club Books, 1983

Sandberg, Graham. *The Exploration of Tibet*. Delhi: Cosmo Publications, 1973

Schaller, George B. *Tibet's Hidden Wilderness*. New York: Abrams, 1997

———. *Wildlife of the Tibetan Steppe*. Chicago and London: University of Chicago Press, 1998

Shelton, Flora Beal. *Sunshine and Shadow on the Tibetan Border*. Cincinnati: Foreign Christian Missionary Society, 1912

Shipton, Eric Earle. *Mountains of Tartary*. London: Hodder and Stoughton, 1951

Sinor, Denis, ed. *The Cambridge History of Early Inner Asia*. Cambridge: Cambridge University Press, 1990

Skrine, Clarmont Percival. *Chinese Central Asia*. London: Methuen, 1926. Reprinted, Hong Kong: Oxford University Press, 1986

Stein, Sir Aurel. *On Central Asian Tracks*. London: Macmillan, 1933. Reprinted, University of Chicago Press, 1964

Strong, Anna Louise. *The Road to the Grey Pamir*. New York: Robert M. McBride, 1931

Sutton, S.B. *In China's Border Provinces*. New York: Hastings House, 1974

Sykes, Ella, and Percy Sykes. *Through Deserts and Oases of Central Asia*. London: Macmillan, 1920

Teichman, Eric. *Journey to Turkistan*. London: Hodder and Stoughton, 1937. Reprinted, Hong Kong: Oxford University Press, 1988

———. *Travels of a Consular Officer in North-west China*. Cambridge: Cambridge University Press, 1921

Wilson, Ernest Henry. *A Naturalist in Western China*. 2 vols. London: Methuen, 1913. Reprinted, London: Cadogan Books, 1986

Winnington, Alan. *The Slaves of the Cool Mountains*. Berlin: Seven Seas, 1962

———. *Tibet: Record of a Journey*. New York: International Publishers, 1957

Wong How-Man. *Exploring the Yangtze, China's Longest River*. San Francisco: China Books and Periodicals, 1989

———. "Peoples of China's Far Provinces." *National Geographic*, Vol. 165, No. 3, March 1984, pp. 283–333

Wong How-Man and Adel A. Dajani. *Islamic Frontiers of China*. Buckhurst Hill: Scorpion, 1990.

Younghusband, Francis E. *The Heart of a Continent*. London: John Murray, 1896

CHINA EXPLORATION
RESEARCH SOCIETY

In 1987, Wong How Man founded the China Exploration and Research Society (CERS) at his home in Los Angeles. In 1994, he moved CERS headquarters to Hong Kong. Born and raised in that former British colony, Wong feels a strong commitment to his Chinese roots and seeks to learn more about mainland China's unique cultures. Working with a team of predominately Chinese scientists, CERS maintains several conservation projects throughout the People's Republic.

The China Exploration and Research Society conducts multi-disciplinary research projects dedicated to both cultural and wildlife conservation in the farthest reaches of China. Research centers in Kunming, Yunnan and Dunhuang, Gansu act as "base camps" for expeditions to each project site, and for additional exploration work.

Wong is most at home as an explorer with CERS, explaining that conservation fills a temporary void in which an increasing number of mainlanders are becoming qualified. However, only those who push themselves to the outer limits can rediscover such remote sites for preservation. Thus, through cooperative projects with local government authorities, CERS seeks to conserve the irreplaceable natural and cultural resources of the People's Republic of China.

Current CERS projects include:
- Silk Road Archaeology, using NASA's shuttle imaging radar
- Conservation in the Arjin Shan Nature Reserve
- Tibetan Monastery Restoration in Western Sichuan
- Black-necked Crane Conservation
- Preservation of Moso Culture: a Matrilineal Village at Luguhu
- Wildlife Conservation in Aksai Kazak Autonomous County
- Hanging Coffins of the Bo People
- Cave Exploration in Yunnan

For more information about the China Exploration and Research Society, please contact:

CERS
B 2308 South Mark, 11 Yip Hing Street
Wong Chuk Hang, Hong Kong
Tel: (852) 2555 7776
Fax: (852) 2555 2661
E-mail: cers@asiaonline.net

1. In Kunming, CERS team prepares for 1995 journey to the Yangtze River's source.

2. Crossing a cantilever bridge on the Tibetan Plateau.

3. We celebrate with Coca-Cola, not champagne, near the source of the Yangtze in 1995. Due to decreased pressure at high altitude, the soda cans "explode" without even being shaken.

4. An angry wild yak charges our Land Rover.

5. Gore-Tex-clad team members pose with Tibetan warriors—and their rifles—in Konkaling, 1997.

6. Wong charts the day's route near the Yangtze source, 1995.

7. A frigid Manchurian winter in 1983: Chen Li and Wong How Man at left.

8. Driving through the vast desert. Note yaks in distance.

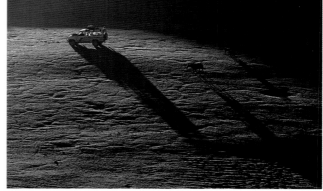

1. A carefully chosen campsite in the Khartan River Valley, Aksai County, 1998.

2. Even the trusty Land Rovers get stuck from time to time.

3. Preparing dinner in camp. Tents provided by The North Face give us a home away from home.

4. Morning snow on car windows, Aksai County, May 1998.

5. Camping near Kazak yurts, Aksai Couty.

6. Summer rains on the Tibetan Plateau can stop traffic for days, until the mud subsides or bulldozers arrive.

7. Wind-eroded sandstone formations, called *yardang*, dwarf our tents in the Xinjiang desert.

8. Treacherous travel during rainy season, Tibet, 1982.

1. Wong uses solar panels to charge his laptop computer.

2. CERS team nurses Tibetan gazelle with broken leg.

3. After a hard day's work, CERS explorers enjoy a hot meal, fired by MSR stoves.

4. A double-humped camel makes the perfect ship of the desert.

5. Testing out a portable decompression chamber to combat the effects of altitude sickness at 3,900 meters (12,795 ft) above sea level, 1998.

6. This yak helped keep my feet dry for frigid river crossings at high altitude during the 1985 search for the source of the Yangtze.

7. Waking to fresh snow cover is commonplace on expeditions, making The North Face down jackets indispensable.

8. Hawking with Kirgiz hunters near Akqi, 1984.

GLOSSARY

akhoi KIRG portable felt tent of the Kirgiz. *See also* yurt.

Altun Tagh MONG "Gold Mountains." Chinese *Arjin Shan*.

Amdo TIB northeastern section of the Tibetan Plateau; historically one of Tibet's three provinces.

argali MONG *Ovis ammon;* wild sheep of the high plateau, prized for its spiralling horns.

argul MONG dried cow, sheep or yak dung, used for fuel in many Asian pastoral areas.

Arjin Shan CHIN mountain range in southeast corner of the Xinjiang Uygur Autonomous Region; home of China's second largest nature reserve.

Bactrian camel double-humped, domestic camel of Central Asia, whose wild cousins still roam the Lop Nor desert.

baigu KIRG traditional game of Inner Asia grasslands, popular among Kirgiz and Kazak. Players on horseback vie for possession of a decapitated sheep or goat; some call this the forerunner of polo.

ba-nag TIB "black tent" of the Tibetan nomad. Usually quadrilateral, the tent is supported by one horizontal and two vertical poles, staked to the ground and pulled out with ropes.

bashi TURK caravan leader.

bharal TURK blue sheep (*Pseudois nayaur*). Tibetan *nawa*.

Bon TIB ancient, animistic tradition prevalent in Tibet before the advent of Buddhism in the seventh century. Because Tibetan Buddhism and Bon adopted many of each other's traditions, their rituals outwardly appear similar.

bordzig MONG sweet, flattened fried dough; a staple of Mongol and Kazak diets.

cham TIB dance dramas performed by monks during religious festivals.

chang TIB strong alcoholic, beer-like beverage made of barley; the Tibetans' national drink.

Changtang TIB "northern plain" of Tibetan Plateau, home to some rare wildlife. Within it is the second largest wildlife refuge in the world, at 330,000 sq km (127,500 sq mi).

chiru TIB Tibetan antelope (*Pantholops hodgsoni*). *See also* shahtoosh.

chorten TIB Tibetan funerary mound (*stupa*) commonly used to mark holy sites and mountain passes. Bulbous in shape, such towers contain reliquaries of highly revered lamas.

chuba TIB basic, full-length robe worn by Tibetans of either sex; made of sheepskin or *pulu*. A belt or sash secures the waist, the right sleeve thrown off in warm weather.

co TIB river.

Dalai Lama MONG, TIB "Ocean of Wisdom." The supreme authority in the Gelukpa sect of Tibetan Buddhism.

damaru TIB hand-held, double-faced drum with clappers on strings that rattle as it is turned, used in Tibetan rituals.

dorje TIB "diamond scepter;" magical weapon used by monks, representing a thunderbolt. Held in the right hand, with a *dril-bu* in the left, this ritual item symbolizes the mystical union of compassion and wisdom.

dril-bu TIB small bronze bell, topped with a half *dorje*, used in Tibetan Buddhist rituals.

drokpa TIB herdsman or nomad; "man of the solitudes."

gawo TIB metal or leather charm box which Tibetans carry with them for protection.

Gelukpa TIB school of Buddhism founded by Tsongkhapa in the 14th century, now prevalent in Tibet and Mongolia; "the virtuous ones." Sometimes called the "Yellow Hat Sect."

ger MONG *see* yurt.

gobi CHIN a desert of small pebbles, generally over a clay base, with scarce rainfall, few wells and sparse vegetation. Much of the desert in northwest China consists of gobi. Not to be confused with the Gobi Desert in Mongolia.

gonpa TIB monastery.

gyaling TIB small, high-pitched trumpet used in Tibetan Buddhist ritual ceremony.

Han CHIN majority ethnic group comprising 92 percent of China's population.

he CHIN river.

Himalayas extensive mountain range stretching 2,414 km (1,500 mi) through south Asia; includes nine of the world's ten highest peaks.

Hump, the a nickname for the Himalayas used by Allied airmen transporting supplies for Chiang Kai-shek's Nationalist regime in World War II.

Kagyupa TIB adherent of the Kagyu school of Tibetan Buddhism; "oral transmission of the doctrine from master to disciple."

kalpak KIRG white, pointed caps, tri-sected by black lines of felt, worn by Kirgiz men and boys.

kalym KAZ bride price, as set by the Kazak bride's father, local judge or priest.

Kham TIB area of eastern Tibet; one of three traditional Tibetan provinces.

Khampa TIB person from eastern Tibet (Kham); notorious as brigands and bandits.

khan MONG "leader," as in Genghis Khan.

khana MONG willow framework for the felt tent (yurt) of Mongols, Kazak and Kirgiz.

khangpa TIB house.

khan-po TIB head lama.

Khartan MONG "Black Hills;" a commonly used Mongol place name.

khata TIB ceremonial white silk scarf used as an offering and greeting.

kiang TIB Tibetan wild ass (*Equus kiang*). Chinese *yelu*.

kumiss TURK an alcoholic drink of fermented mare's milk, served by Mongol, Kirgiz and Kazak nomads; Mongolian *airag*.

la TIB mountain pass.

lakto TIB yak driver; "hand with a stone."

lama TIB Buddhist priest or spiritual mentor.

Lung ta TIB Tibetan prayer mantras printed on cloth or paper, released into the air at mountain passes for good luck; "wind horse."

mani TIB prayer, rosary.

mantra SAN mystic incantations repeated as a form of Buddhist practice.

Monlam Chenmo TIB Great Prayer Festival held in Lhasa during first month of the lunar year.

naan leavened flat bread of flour and cornmeal, usually baked on a vertical oven wall.

nor MONG lake.

nyan TIB Tibetan horned god of the earth. *See also* argali.

Nyingmapa TIB adherent of the Nyingma school of Tibetan Buddhism; "those of the ancient teachings;" the oldest order of Tibetan Buddhism.

Om Mani Padme Hum TIB literally, "Hail the Jewel in the Lotus!" This sacred mantra invokes Shenrezi, the God of Compassion.

Pamir roof of the world in southern Central Asia, where the Himalayan, Karakoram and Kunlun Mountains converge; Khokandese "desert."

paozi CHIN Eurasian roe deer (*Capreolus capreolus*).

pulu TIB heavy woolen cloth prized throughout Tibet and Mongolia; made into traditional robes, called *chuba*.

ragdong TIB large, deep-toned trumpet; an instrument in Tibetan orchestras.

rinpoche TIB an incarnate lama; "high in value or esteem."

shahtoosh PERS "king of wool;" warmest, most luxurious wool in the world, woven into shawls in India to supply the world's fashion markets.

shan CHIN mountain.

Shanag Cham TIB Black Hat Dance performed for the Great Prayer Festival.

shaoshu minzu CHIN "minority nationality." China officially recognizes 55 ethnic nationalities, who comprise eight percent of the population and occupy 65 percent of the land area.

Shenrezi TIB patron deity of Tibetan Buddhism. Tibetans believe the Dalai Lama to be Shenrezi's incarnation.

si CHIN monastery.

Songtsen Gampo TIB king responsible for seventh-century introduction of Buddhism to Tibet.

Taklamakan TURK "go in and do not come out," the Taklamakan Desert in southern Xinjiang.

tangka TIB portable religious scroll painting on treated cotton or silk, hung from ceilings or walls of monasteries; traditionally painted in bright colors, with natural ground mineral and vegetable substances.

Tibetan Buddhism religion practiced in Tibetan and Mongolian areas, imported to Tibet from India under Songtsen Gampo, AD 630.

torma TIB butter sculpture.

trapa TIB student monk.

tsampa TIB parched, ground barley meal lightly roasted; staple food for all Tibetans.

tsarwa YI woolen cape used as both jacket and bedding.

tulku TIB living Buddha; a lama of high rank.

xierenzhu CHIN tipi-like structure used by Yagut people in Manchuria, covered with birch bark or animal hides.

yak TIB cow-like animal (*Bos grunniens*) of the steppe. Domestic yak provide Tibetans with transport, food, clothing and shelter. Also wild yak.

yurt TURK portable, domed tent used by Central Asian nomads; Mongolian *ger*.

zu CHIN nation, nationality or ethnic group.

INDEX